iN GUIDE NEW YORK

At the beginning of the 17th century, when European capitals like London and Paris had long reached the status of world cities, New York was still an unknown village. It was not until the late 18th century that the former Nieuw Amsterdam grew into an important economic and financial metropolis. This is when the city became an important refuge for many immigrants. New York stood synonymous with hope and an optimism that inspired rich and poor alike; the lights on Times Square, Broadway, the Empire State Building, temples of culture such as the Met and the MoMA, a sea of yellow cabs, and at the port entrance the Statue of Liberty, the symbol of freedom. During the course of its history, New York has experienced many setbacks, yet even in the bleakest hours the city could count on the unwavering dynamism and the pioneering spirirt of its inhabitants, the New Yorkers.

InGuide New York is illustrated with stunning photographs as you would expect to find in a large coffee-table book yet it is also a highly informative travel guidebook. Area by area, images and vivid descriptions introduce all the important sights, revealing many amazing facts about the city and its people, its art and culture, the everyday and the unusual. "Compact New York", has insider tips which identify the best restaurants, hotels, and shops, as well as the trendiest neighborhoods, important addresses, and useful facts. Another chapter introduces the top museums in detailed descriptions and images. Finally, the City Walks are packed with shopping and dining tips that will inspire you to explore New York's boroughs and areas. A detailed, removable city map completes this unique picture travel guide. It makes it easy for you to find all the city's highlights by grid reference.

CONTENTS

Left: view of the skyline in southern Manhattan seen from Brooklyn Heights
Previous pages: on the "Top of the Rock" viewing platform in the Rockefeller Center, and on Times Square.

New Yorkers know ups and downs not just as a measure of moods but also in geographical terms: Uptown is the northern part of Manhattan, whereas Downtown stretches to the southern tip.

New York City is not just divided into five boroughs – Manhattan, Brooklyn, Queens, The Bronx, and Staten Island – but also into 59 Community Boards with districts such as Greenwich Village and SoHo, which is why New York has often been called a "city of neighborhoods". Sandwiched between the Atlantic estuary of the East River and the Hudson River, Manhattan Island is neatly divided into Downtown (stretching from the island's southern tip to 30th Street), Midtown (from 30th Street to Central Park) and Uptown (from Central Park and north, into Harlem and Washington Heights).

The Statue of Liberty, New York's most iconic monument, is actually French. It was conceived at a dinner party in 1865 in Paris, when the political activist Edouard René Lefebvre de Laboulaye and the sculptor Frédéric-Auguste Bartholdi railed against the rule of Napoleon III. In an effort to anger the ruler they came up with the idea of gifting a statue to the United States. Inspired by the Colossus of Rhodes, it was constructed in France, then dismantled and transported by sea to America in crates. It was unveiled on its site on Liberty Island in New York Harbor on October 28

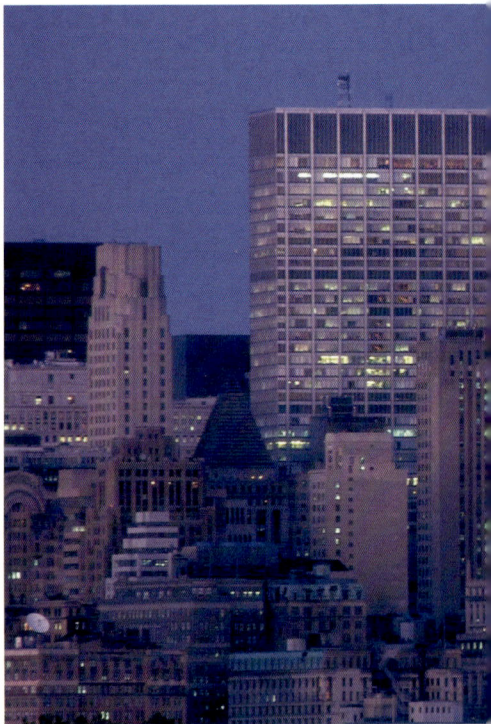

Located off Manhattan's southern tip, at the harbor entrance to New York City (large picture) are Ellis Island (top right) and Liberty Island with the word-famous Statue of Liberty. More than 15 million people have entered the United States via Ellis Island since 1892 (above). The original building and a museum commemorate the era of immigration.

1886. Now a UNESCO World Heritage Site, the statue's foundations weigh 24,000 tons and her robes conceal a steel frame buult by Alexandre Gustav Eiffel. Every immigrant arriving between 1892 and 1954 to seek a new life in America was processed at Ellis Island at the mouth of the Hudson River.

The Staten Island Ferry connects the southern tip of Manhattan with Staten Island, which lies in the bay. About 200 million passengers a year travel between South Ferry (Whitehall Street) and St George Ferry Terminal. In the 18th century two private sailboats covered the short trip, and in the 19th century the first steamships arrived. There was a disaster in 1871, when the Westfield's boiler exploded, killing 85 people. The ferries have been owned and operated by the City of New York since 1905. In 1897, the 20-minute crossing cost five cents, and the price was not changed until 1972,

The ferry service runs 24 hours a day between Manhattan and Staten Island and is used by about 20 million people annually, both commuters and visitors to New York. The ships are painted bright orange so they can be seen more clearly in fog.

when it was raised to 10 cents. In 1975 it was increased to 25 cents, and in 1990 to 50 cents, but since 1997, the journey has been free for foot passengers. There isn't a better sightseeing tour of downtown Manhattan – the ferry has magnificent views of the city's skyline and its bridges.

The current Trinity Church, built in 1846 to a neo-Gothic design by Richard Upjohn, was preceded by a series of Anglican churches: the first was built as early as 1698, but burnt down eight years later, in 1706. A second church constructed on the site and consecrated in 1790, was demolished in 1839 for safety reasons. The modern bronze doors are reminiscent of Lorenzo Ghiberti's "*Gates of Paradise*" for the Baptistry in Florence. A bronze by Steve Tobin was placed in front of the church in 2005 to commemorate the tragic events of 9/11. Parts of the church's historic cemetery date back to

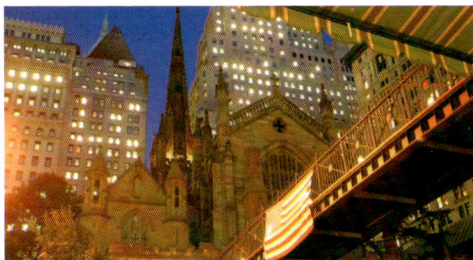

the 18th century, and it includes the graves of Alexander Hamilton, the first US Secretary of the Treasury, and Robert Fulton, the inventor of the steamship. The church has a museum that hosts special exhibitions throughout the year illustrating the history of New York and of the parish.

Tradition meets modernity: The sandstone building of Trinity Church (top) is hemmed in amongst the skyscrapers of the Financial District. Above: One of the Biblical scenes depicted on the bronze doors by Richard Morris. Large picture: The interior of the three-nave basilica.

The heart of New York's Financial District is Wall Street, which runs along the site of a wooden defensive wall erected by the Dutch in 1653 to protect themselves from attack. Alexander Hamilton, the country's first Secretary of the Treasury, established New York as a headquarters for stock trading and issued federal government bonds to offset the debts incurred during the War of Independence. Although Wall Street became synonymous with finance, the Stock Exchange is located round the corner, on Broad Street, between Wall Street and Exchange Place. In 1936, a marble relief entitled

The neo-classical façade of the New York Stock Exchange, designed by George B. Post in 1903, is reminiscent of a Greek temple. The statue of George Washington seems to keep a close eye on things (large picture). Until 2005, the traders in the New Yorker Stock Exchange communicated by shouting at each other across the floor, until an electronic trading system was installed (top right).

"*Integrity Protecting the Works of Man*", was placed above the Corinthian pillars of the façade, representing the Stock Exchange as the index of the nation's wealth. Integrity stands in the center, with Agriculture and Mining, to the left and Science, Industry, and Invention, to the right.

On 17 May 1792, 24 business-men and bankers met under a plane tree on Wall Street and signed an agreement to regulate the purchase and sale of shares and bonds, laying the foundations for the New York Stock Exchange. The "New York Stock & Exchange Board" extended and formalized these revolutionary rules in 1817, and the current title of the "New York Stock Exchange" was finally adopted in 1863. In the first few years, two sessions were held, in which the president of the exchange would call out the stocks, and members submitted their offers. Each member had their own chair, or "seat", and in 1817 this privilege cost just $25. The NYSE is currently the largest stock exchange in the world. It has been state-regulated since 1934 and is run by a private corporation of stock brokers and traders; the oldest stock index is the Dow Jones Index. Listed on the

THE WORLD'S FINANCIAL CENTER

stock market since 2006 as the NYSE Group, the concern created "NYSE Euronext, Inc", the world's first transatlantic stock exchange, in a merger in April 2007. The acquisition of the American Stock Exchange (AMEX) in October 2008 gave rise to the formation of the "NYSE Alternext US".

Because of the importance attached to New York as the financial capital of the world traders need to keep an eye on the global markets (large picture). The free convertibility of the U.S. dollar (above), that is the right for unrestricted currency exchange guaranteed by the U.S. Central Bank, facilitates the worldwide trade. Top: Arturo Di Modica's sculpture, *Charging Bull*, is meant to spread optimism among traders.

Excavations for the World Trade Center produced enough spoil to create a strip of shoreline on which Battery Park City was built. The hub of the complex, built in the second half of the 1980s to designs by César Palli, is the World Financial Center: four granite and glass office blocks of differing heights, with up to 51 floors and post-modern copper roofs. Each building reflects a basic architectural form: a truncated pyramid, a cupola, a pyramid, and a ziggurat (stepped pyramid). The façades of towers two and three were badly damaged during the attack on the World Trade Center in

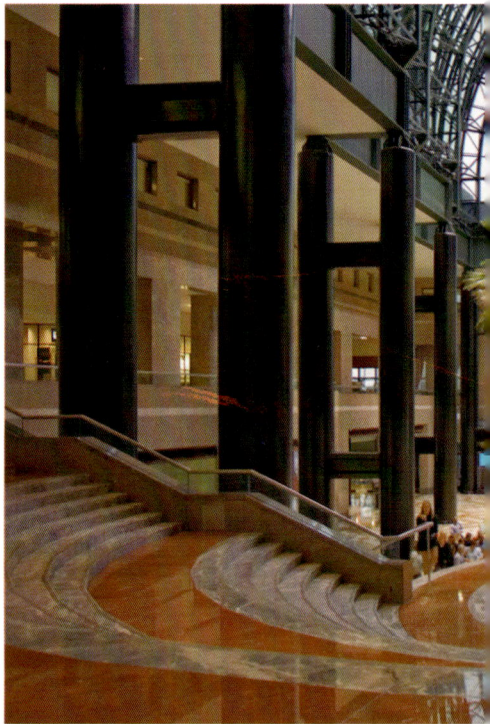

There is a yawning gap between the towers of the World Financial Center (top right), and the Hudson River marina) where the Twin Towers of the World Trade Center once stood. At the heart of the complex, which was celebrated as the Rockefeller Center of the 21st Century during its inauguration in 1988, is a large conservatory with shops and restaurants. Sixteen royal palms from the Mojave Desert create an exotic atmosphere (large picture).

WORLD FINANCIAL CENTER (WFC) 6

2001, but they were soon repaired. The WFC has a total area of 27,000 sq. m (291,000 sq. ft) and is home to financial giants such as Dow Jones and American Express. It also hosts free arts events, plays, and concerts. The open plaza has a view of the Hudson River and North Cove Yacht Harbor.

Built on square foundations to heights of 415 m (1,361 ft) and 417m (1,368 ft) respectively, the stainless steel Twin Towers of the World Trade Center were, for a few weeks after their completion in 1974, the tallest buildings in the world, only ceding this crown to the 443-m (1,453-ft) high Sears Tower in Chicago. The Twin Towers, each with 110 floors, were part of a complex of seven office buildings that were connected to the World Financial Center by underground passages and by a bridge. Known as Ground Zero since the attack of September 11, 2001, the 6.5-ha (16-acre) site was not completely cleared

of rubble from the towers until the summer of 2002. It was originally planned that five new skyscrapers were to be built here, but the financial crises of 2009 led to revisions and/or the shelving to these plans. There is also a controversial plan to build an Islamic community center and mosque.

"Tribute in Light" – each year on September 11, the attack is commemorated (above; large picture and top: Ground Zero building site): "I've seen a lot of things, but the worst thing about being ... there was that you couldn't see anything. No bodies, no computers, no telephones, no doors, not even a door handle. Do you know how many ... handles there were in the World Trade Centre?" (Sal D'Agonstino, firefighter).

St Paul's Chapel, in which George Washington once worshiped, was completed in 1776 and is New York's oldest church. It was created by master craftsman Andrew Gautier who probably based the design on James Gibbs's church of St Martin's in the Fields in London. Apart from the addition of a spire in 1796, the building has remained unchanged since its consecration. During the rubble clearing after the attacks of September 11, 2001, this Episcopal chapel (which belongs to the Anglican church) was used by workers to rest. Miraculously, the church was not destroyed

The World Trade Center, situated right behind the old cemetery (above) on the west side of St Paul's Chapel (large picture and top right), was destroyed on September 11, 2001. The terror attacks turned the sacred building into a solemn place of remembrance.

during the attack: a nearby tree dissipated the effects of the shockwaves so completely that not even a windowpane was broken. Only a stump and the roots of the protective tree survived, inspiring the sculpture which now stands in front of Trinity Church – *Trinity Root* created by Steve Tobin.

The old port area between Water Street and the East River is now a listed historic district. In the middle of the 1960s, a group of citizens calling themselves the "South Street Museum" began collecting boats and buying up dilapidated buildings in the port area. About ten years later, the notion arose of transforming the area into a living district and tourist attraction, with restored and new buildings, museums, stores, and historical sailing vessels, including the Flying P-Liner, Peking, some of which could house museums themselves. Schermerhorn Row, with its 1813 warehouses and

The East River connects Long Island Sound with New York Bay. The pull of the tides causes the water to flow so fast that even in winter, ice cannot form. This explains the importance of the bay as an anchorage in the days of wooden tall ships (top right: the four-masted Peking). The Fulton Market Building (large picture) commemorates the fish market of the same name, which moved to the Bronx in 2005.

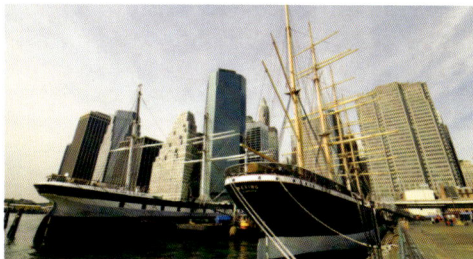

offices, is the pride of the port. The Fulton Fish Market has become a shopping mall and a small lighthouse commemorating the sinking of the Titanic in 1912. Pier 17 has three floors of restaurants and stores, and a fantastic view of Brooklyn Bridge, the East River, and Brooklyn Heights.

This legendary bridge, spanning the East River between Manhattan and Brooklyn, was opened in May 1883 after 16 years of construction. Not including the approach roads, it is 1,052 m (3,451 ft) in length; including the approach roads 1,825 m (5,987 ft). Its first day of service saw 150,000 people cross the bridge. To convince contemporary skeptics of the structure's stability, Barnum's Circus sent an entire herd of elephants over the bridge. Designing the Brooklyn Bridge was originally the responsibility of the German architect, John Augustus Roebling, but he died

When it was unveiled, the Brooklyn Bridge was hailed as a miracle of engineering and was the longest suspension bridge in the world (large picture). The "Elevated Pleasure Walk", a wooden pedestrian path above the road (top right), was designed for walkers – certainly the most beautiful promenade in the city.

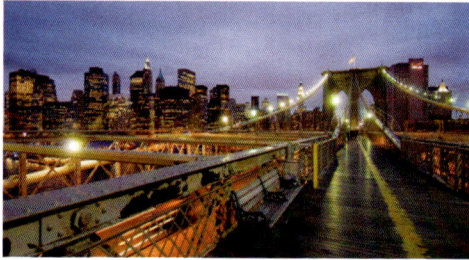

shortly after construction began. His son Washington took on the challenge together with his wife, Emily, and supervised the work. The Brooklyn Bridge was the first suspension bridge in the world to incorporate steel wires: around 24,000 km (15,000 miles) of wire was used on the bridge.

On its unveiling in April 1913, the Woolworth Building was hailed as the "eighth wonder of the world". At 241 m (790 ft) in height it was the world's tallest building (until 1930) and the man who commissioned it, Franklin Winfield Woolworth, never omitted to mention that he had paid for it – all $13.5 million's worth – in cash. His rise to department store king had begun with a "five cent store" in Utica, New York. When this went bust he tried his luck in Lancaster, Pennsylvania, extending his range to include goods that also cost a dime. He opened his first store in New York in 1896

and at the time of his death, in 1916, he owned an empire of more than a thousand stores around the world and had also amassed a personal fortune of $65 million. A relief of him – counting his money – can be found in the lobby of the Woolworth Building, the so-called "Cathedral of Commerce".

The Woolworth Building (large picture: seen from the City Hall Park; above: the roof; top: the lobby) was described as the "Cathedral of Commerce", but according to the architect, Cass Gilbert, it was based on Gothic town halls rather than church architecture.

DOWNTOWN MANHATTAN

South of Chinatown, bounded to the west by Broadway and to the east by the East River, lies New York's legal and administrative district – the Civic Center. Its many public buildings include City Hall, the oldest in the United States, which is still the headquarters of the city's administration today. It is now listed and protected as an historic place. It was constructed between 1803 and 1812 by Joseph François Mangin and John McComb Jr in the "Federal Style" that developed out of the British Colonial Style after the War of Independence. The City Hall Park alongside the building had been open ground in the

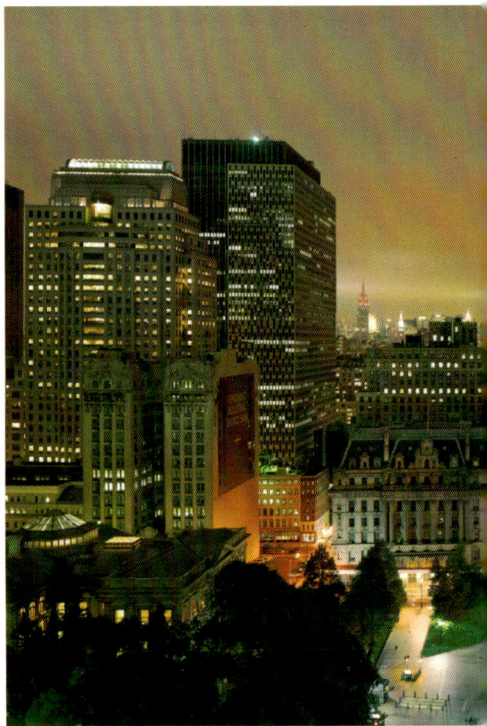

The Municipal Building towers over the Civic Center (large picture). Its dome is an architectural reference to the much smaller City Hall. It is crowned by a gilded statue called *Civic Fame* – this was erected in March 1913 in celebration of the union of the five boroughs into one city. Opposite the City Hall, a monument commemorates Nathan Hale, who was hanged in Britain in 1776 as the "first spy from America" (top right).

18th century, used for grazing cattle, as an assembly point, and for military exercises. The Municipal Building, an office block completed in 1914 to accommodate increased space needed for city administrators, provides an architectural contrast to City Hall. The area now also includes many upscale residential blocks.

TriBeCa (the "Triangle Below Canal Street") is another example of how New York continually reinvents itself. In the mid-1970s this was a run-down industrial area known as the "Lower West Side", until a property developer recognized the potential of its many empty factories and warehouses and, in the process, also invented the new abbreviation. His gamble paid off: TriBeCa was suddenly "cool" and many artists from nearby SoHo relocated their ateliers, studios, and rehearsal rooms in the area as the rents were still relatively cheap. It is here that loft conversions took off in

Hollywood star Robert de Niro has done a lot for TriBeCa (above: one of the typical narrow streets between houses). He was the driving force behind the annual TriBeCa Film Festival; he's the co-owner of the Tribeca Grill (large picture); and he was also a partner in Nobu Matsuhisa (top right: the Nobu New York), bringing the finest Japanese cuisine to TriBe-Ca, a restaurant that has earned a Michelin star.

a big way. TriBeCa is still chic and trendy but now also very expensive, so the in-crowd has long since moved out. The triangle of streets between West Broadway, Canal West, and Chambers Street now boasts more restaurants than galleries – including some of the best in the New York City.

DOWNTOWN MANHATTAN

The Chinese enclave south of Canal Street is now home to around 200,000 Chinese people, the largest Asian community outside that continent. All the signs are written in Chinese characters and the aroma of Peking duck and exotic sauces wafts from the open doorways. Thanks to its 200-plus restaurants, over 300 flourishing textile and clothing firms, numerous shops and grocery stores, and seven daily Chinese newspapers, Chinatown is an independent metropolis within Manhattan. The Buddhist Temple of America is located on Mott Street and the Church of the Transfiguration,

Manhattan's Chinatown grew up in the 1870s, between Canal, Baxter, Worth, and Park streets, and the Bowery, but it has long moved beyond this area and is now a "city within a city". In the north it has started encroaching on large parts of Little Italy; it has almost reached SoHo, and on the Lower East Side, once the home of the Jewish community, more Mandarin and Cantonese can be heard than English.

built in 1801 and Roman Catholic since 1850 (once an important focus for Irish and Italian immigrants) has had a Chinese priest since 1970. The infamous "Bloody Angle", the scene of past skirmishes between opposing Chinese gangs (known as the "Tong Wars"), can be found on Doyers Street.

According to former mayor, Ed Koch, an artist's role in New York is "to make a district so attractive that the artists can't afford to live there any more". And the real estate broker's job, one might add, is to package it attractively: just like TriBeCa, the abbreviation SoHo ("South of Houston") has com-mercial roots, referring to an industrial area south of Houston Street once known as the "South Village". In the 1960s the area, which had become dilapidated, started to attract artists and bohemians. They quickly moved into the empty loft spaces and long-deserted factory buildings – at least

Thumbs up for the district (large picture): Visitors will probably meet up under a fire escape before going to the galleries and wacky antiques stores. The most interesting shops are on Prince Street (top right: Prada), on West Broadway, and in Spring Street. Water tanks (above) also feature on brand-new houses: they are needed because the pressure in New York's water pipes is not sufficient to supply the upper floors.

until Ed Koch's prediction was fulfilled. SoHo is now a trendy locale famous for its style and destination shopping. It's a great place for exploring antique stores and unusual galleries, such as the Guggenheim Soho, and to admire its unique and wonderful streets of cast-iron architecture.

SoHo's streets also have a long tradition of combining art and architecture. However, it is a design style that was neglected until the 1960s, and would have dwindled to nothing had conservationists not realized the rarity value of the cast-iron houses which are common here. Many have now been restored. Cast iron became a popular building material in the 19th century because it was lighter and cheaper to work than stone or brick, and it permitted the architect to prefabricate decorations and façades in the foundry and then have them bolted together on site like plates. Cast iron was also prized for its fire resistance. The era of cast-iron buildings only really ended with the construction of steel-framed skyscrapers in the 1890s, and New York retains the world's greatest concentration of façades wholly or partly constructed of cast iron. The most beautiful houses are,

ART AND ARCHITECTURE
IN A CAST-IRON FRAME

unsurprisingly, in the SoHo Cast Iron Historic District, between West Broadway, West Houston Street, Canal Street, and Crosby Street which became a National Historic Landmark in 1978. Green Street, at its heart, has over 50 buildings spread across five blocks, all built between 1869 and 1895.

Appearances can be deceptive: in SoHo, what looks like marble, brick, or sandstone is usually cast iron (large picture: on West Broadway; top: in the Cast Iron Historic District). One of SoHo's architectural monuments is the Singer Building (above) with its beautiful filigree-design ornamentation.

"I grew up in a world which was more European than American", the director Martin Scorsese once said; like his acting alter ego, Robert de Niro, he grew up in Little Italy. Scorsese's grand-parents, who partly brought him up, were illiterate Sicilian peasants who spoke no English and who, like many southern Italians in the 19th century, had left real poverty to emigrate to New York, where some 40,000 Italians lived in a district stretching from Canal Street to Houston Street. A world of its own, it now exists only in films. Modern-day Little Italy is amongst Manhattan's smallest

Among the Italian restaurants in New York with the longest tradition are the Puglia in Hester Street (large picture), and Lombardi's (top right), the first pizzeria in the United States (1905). Some stores (above) still have the charm of an Italian quarter. In Mulberry, Mott, Grand, and Broome streets, the aroma of pasta wafts through the air. The patron saint of Naples is celebrated at the Feast of San Gennaro in September.

ethnic quarters, with only about 5,000 Italians living in about four blocks; the rest have moved on, to Brooklyn or the Bronx. There are, however, numerous Italian food stores and restaurants here, and in September, many Italians still congregate for the 11-day Feast of San Gennaro.

At the beginning of the 20th century, Manhattan's Lower East Side, the district between the Bowery and Clinton Street, East Houston, and Canal Street, had been settled by the world's largest Jewish community. These Eastern European immigrants lived in generally appalling conditions in six or seven-floor tenements. They were often squashed into tiny, windowless rooms, sharing dirty, dilapidated kitchens and rusty washbasins, with a single toilet outside in the hall. It was so unbearably hot in summer that many residents slept on the roof. The Tenement Museum in Orchard Street comme-

Eldridge Street synagogue, in the street of the same name, is a reminder of the Lower East Side's Jewish roots (above). When it was built in 1887 by Eastern European Orthodox Ashkenazi Jews, it was the most magnificent synagogue in the district; it was restored in 2007. Little remains in the Lower East Side to remind us of older days; the area is now predominantly inhabited by peope of Hispanic and Asian descent.

morates the awful conditions experienced by the immigrants on the Lower East Side. The district still has some 300 synagogues and a few Jewish stores, but most of New York's Jewish population live outside Manhattan. Today, the Lower East Side is home to many Puerto Ricans and Dominicans.

The north part of the Lower East Side was already known as the "East Village" by the 1950s, and nowadays the area east of Broadway between 14th and Houston Street bears the name. The district where Peter Stuyvesant had once owned land was first inhabited by the elite – the Astors and the Vanderbilts of 19th-century New York high society. Immigrants of various nationalities later moved into the area, which became a home for beatniks and would-be beatniks in the middle of the 20th century. Allen Ginsberg, Jack Kerouac, and other such literary giants gave readings

wherever a podium could be found, and John Coltrane played his heart out in smoky jazz clubs. The hippies followed, succeeded by punks, and even today the East Village, where artists such as Keith Haring and Jeff Koons first came to prominence, wecomes the authentically avant-garde.

The eastern part of the East Village which contains "Alpha-bet City", consisting of Avenues A, B, and C, is one of the most fashionable areas of the city. (top the intersection of 3rd Avenue and 13th Street; large picture and above: three snap-shots of daily life).

New Yorkers call the area between 14th Street and Houston Street, Hudson River and Broadway Greenwich Village – or just "the Village" for short – and the district's winding, tree-lined streets and picturesque alleys still give the impression of a 17th century hamlet. In 1822, the area ex- panded rapidly when many New Yorkers escaping a yellow fever epidemic further south sought refuge in Greenwich Village and quickly settled down. However, 13 years later, in 1835, it could still claim to be "the ideal of peaceful and respectable living", if Henry James's description in his short

novel, *Washington Square*, published in 1880 is to be believed. The author, whose grandmother lived in the Village, said: "This area ... has a riper, richer, more honorable look [than other wealthy neighborhoods] ... the look of having had something of a social history."

Idyllic spaces in the city: A stroll through Greenwich Village reveals a range of attractive terraced houses in tree-lined streets (large picture and above). Top: From the north side of Washington Square, where it ends, into Fifth Avenue, the view extends to the Washington Square Arch and as far as the nearby skyscrapers right up to the Empire State Building in Midtown.

Greenwich Village became the hub of the sub-culture in the 20th century. The *Village Voice*, the city's first alternative weekly newspaper, was founded by Dan Wolf, Ed Fancher, and Norman Mailer in a two-roomed apartment in 1955. Six years later, in July 1961, one Robert Allen Zimmerman first came to the area; calling himself Bob Dylan, the singer-songwriter found in the intellectual climate of New York University, for whose students Washington Square is almost an annex to the campus, the same sympathetic hearing it had afforded the poets of the "Beat Generation". A lively

nightlife developed around Bleecker Street, and the first gay and lesbian movement began on the internationally famous Christopher Street. Film stars such as Gwyneth Paltrow and Sarah Jessica Parker have both set up home in this still very exciting neighborhood.

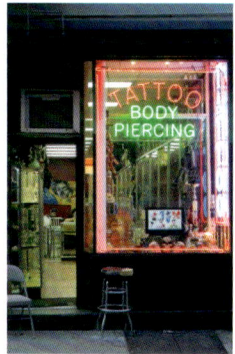

Whether you want a tattoo, or body piercing (above), or just consult a clairvoyant (large picture) – the Village has it all and more. Just walk up the Avenue of the Americas (top) and peep down one of the side-streets.

In the first few decades of the 20th century, the Village became a creative melting pot for all those who tried to find their fortune and happiness outside the accepted norms of society – whether in the field of politics like John Reed who went on to create the first Communist party of the United States, or in the artistic arena like the French artist, Marcel Duchamp, a pioneer of the Dadaist and Surrealist movements. The latter is said to have climbed up the Arch on Washington Square on a cold winter evening, on January 23 1917, together with a group of self-styled bohemians. They

Washington Square is not just the geographical, but also the emotional heart of the area and all sorts of people feel at home there (top right). Here stands the Washington Square Arch, built in 1889 on the occasion of the centenary of George Washington's inauguration and modeled on the Arc de Triomphe in Paris (large picture). At first a wood and plaster construction, the triumphal arch was soon replaced by a marble one.

then celebrated a very special kind of "Tea Party", during which they fired toy pistols and declared festively, in the light of candle lampions, the "Free and Independent Republic of Washington Square". They also appealed to President, Woodrow Wilson to protect their new republic.

Rosy-cheeked women with giant busts, luminous skeletons and scary ghosts, fabulous animals and dragons, garish drag queens and dancing princes, screaming witches and grinning devils: the Village Halloween Parade has become to Manhattan what Carnival is to Rio. Every year on October 31, more than 50,000 masked New Yorkers and an estimated two million visitors celebrate the spirits' return; according to Celtic legend, they are allowed to pass among the living only on Halloween. And they do! The first parade in October 1973 was just a small procession organized by a company making masks in Greenwich Village. The following year, after the Theater for the New City became involved, several thousand masked people were singing and dancing on Sixth Avenue, and since 1975, the Village Halloween Parade has been a spectacular event.

FUN AND GAMES:
THE VILLAGE HALLOWEEN PARADE

Merry New Yorkers in the oddest costumes follow giant "puppets" made of plastic and papier-mâché, dancing to cheerful rhythms supplied by a wide variety of bands. Even after 9/11, New Yorkers refused to miss out on the parade, and the theme that year was the phoenix, rising from the ashes.

The pagan festival of All Hallows' Eve has turned into Halloween, and the whole town seems to dress up for the occasion. Even the cops put on a good face for the sometimes decidedly adult entertainment This might be connected with the Celtic belief that the souls who have died in the last year are allowed to return home for a brief period only, so the celebrations will soon be over...

Before June 28 1969, gays and lesbians had to hide their sexuality; in most bars and cafés they were even less welcome than non-whites. Of all people, it was the Mafia who improved the situation, buying the Stonewall Inn on Christopher Street and turning it into a gay and lesbian bar. Everything was done very discreetly, of course: a bouncer inspected new arrivals through a peephole; "club membership" had to be taken out if visitors wanted to buy alcohol, and no resistance was offered to the monthly police raids – at least not until June 28 1969. During that raid, gays and lesbians took to the streets and openly resisted the police for the first time. They sang *We Shall Overcome*, the anthem of the black civil rights movement, and found a new self-image: Gay Pride. The first gay and lesbian parade to Central Park took place in the summer of 1970, and now

GAY PRIDE: NEW YORK OVER THE RAINBOW

"Christopher Street Day" is now celebrated round the world, flying the rainbow flag as the symbol of gay and lesbian lifestyles. In some countries, it is marked as Gay Pride day, usually held on the last Saturday of June. Stonewall Inn at 51 Christopher Street, is now a listed building.

"Strip him, bathe him, and bring him to my tent", as Cher is reported to have said in her wilder days, when she saw someone she liked. It's certainly possible that her double in *Lips* on Bank Street was thinking of this when preparing her act (large picture; above: "Whitney Houston"). Top: George Segal's *Gay Liberation Monument* of two same-sex couples in Christopher Park.

The name refers to the "union" of two streets: Broadway and the Bowery and had no link with the trade union movement. However, since the days of the American Civil War (1861–1865) it has frequently been used as a location for political events and demonstrations. In the first decade of the 20th century it even had a Speakers' Corner established following the model of the one in London's Hyde Park. In the 19th century, the Square was a tranquil garden in private ownership, but has now developed as a focal point of urban life where employees spend their lunch breaks, young roller

skaters perform their daring feats, and regular markets take place four days every week, offering local organic produce. including delicious apple pies. At Union Square West, Andy Warhol opened his infamous "Factory" art studios from 1962 until 1968, a hippy hangout for arty types.

Henry Kirke Brown designed the equestrian statue of George Washington (top) in the Square in 1856. The local farmers' market (large picture and above) is one of the most popular. At one time the first American film studios were set up around the square – an East Coast Hollywood during the days of silent films. The studios later moved to Los Angeles only because of its milder winter climate.

In the early 1830s, the investor, Samuel B Rugglers, built 66 residential houses on land around a central green space which had once been a swamp. He planted flowers, shrubs and trees and created an idyllic green area. Access to the park was only to the future residents of the complex. What initially was mainly a clever marketing ploy secured an exceptional status for Gramercy Park; today, it's the only private park in New York. This was and still is a very exclusive place to live: Samuel J Tilden, who was elected governor of New York in 1874, moved into 15 Gramercy Park South (since

1906 it has been the home of the National Arts Club); No. 16 was occupied by The Players Club, a private association for people connected with the stage. Since its expansion in 1988, the area extended from East 18th to beyond 21st Street, and in 1966 it was declared an Historic District.

Today, it is still only the residents of the attractive brownstone houses around the Gramercy Park (top) who have right of access to the green space. There's just one exception: the guests of the Gramercy Park Hotel (large picture and above) opened in 1925, where Humphrey Bogart once got married. Built by Robert T Lyons and converted by Ian Schrager: the hotel's lobby now resembles an art gallery.

This park, which sits between Fifth and Madison Avenues, and 23rd and 26th streets, has been a green refuge for New Yorkers since 1686. It was named after James Madison (1751–1836), the fourth president of the United States, and became a public park in 1847. Two years earlier, in 1845, Alexander Cartwright founded the New York Knickerbockers here, the first officially documented baseball club, and Madison Square Park is still regarded by many as the birthplace of this national sport. The park remained at the northern limit of Manhattan up to the population explosion

after the end of the Civil War. Neglected for a long time, the park was comprehensively renovated in the early 21st century by the Madison Square Park Conversancy which invested six million dollars from public and private coffers to create its present function as a beautiful city oasis.

All around the park (above, a statue of governor William H Seward) you'll find architectural icons such as the Metropolitan Life Insurance Building (top); with its tower modeled on the Campanile in Venice, it was the tallest building in the world for four years (1909–1913). In 1876 the arm and the torch of the Statue of Liberty were displayed in the park (large picture) for six years in order to raise funds for the monument's construction.

The Flatiron Building was originally called the Fuller Building and caused a sensation when it was completed in 1902. The architects, Daniel Burnham and John Wellborn Root, had used the wedge-shaped parcel of land at the intersection of 23rd Street, Fifth Avenue, and Broadway to the full, erecting a similarly wedge-shaped skyscraper with a steel frame—a revolutionary design for the time. Clad in light limestone and terracotta, and only 2 m (6.5 ft) wide at its front, the building resembled a giant smoothing iron and was known as the "Flatiron Building" ever after. Its shape, crea-

ted by Broadway's diagonal course through an otherwise grid-shaped city plan, has meant that this 86-m (282-ft) high building of 22 floors has remained one of the best-known and most photographed skyscrapers in New York, and one of the city's most iconic landmarks.

The Flatiron Building achieved its iconic status without any superlatives; it was never the highest building in the city. Its fascination lay entirely in its external shape.

In the middle of the 18th century, Chelsea was a farm belonging to a retired English marine officer, Captain Thomas Clarke, who had named it after the district in London where the famous Royal Military Hospital is located. Nowadays, this area, bounded by 14th and 34th Streets, and Sixth Avenue and the Hudson River, is one of the most attractive and desirable addresses in New York. Chelsea's historic charm, some of which is still apparent today, is mostly due to the writer Clement Clarke Moore. The grandson of Thomas Clarke, he inherited the land and sold it on according to a mainly

The lovingly restored, listed buildings of the row houses in the Chelsea Historic District (top; large picture: a view of the area), dating from the middle of the 19th century, are worth seeing. Their name comes from the brown sandstone building material. Leonard Cohan had an affair with Janis Joplin at the legendary Chelsea Hotel (above.) The latest attraction is the High Line Park – a green oasis one the path of an old train line (top right).

not-for-profit, commerce-free, family-friendly, building policy. The results were, and indeed still are, unmistakable: the pretty terraces in the Chelsea Historic District have been acclaimed as the best in New York. Many artists moved here from SoHo, making it a global center of contemporary art.

Chelsea also has a musical past: at the beginning of the 20th century, most of the music publishing houses in the United States had their offices on 28th Street, all working industriously on the *Great American Songbook*. The *New York Herald* journalist, Monroe Rosenfeld, likened the tinkling of the practice pianos, which could be heard out on the street, to tin pans being knocked together, and so he named the street "Tin Pan Alley". The Chelsea Piers – four landing stages between 17th and 23rd Streets – stretch out into the Hudson River like fingers, a reminder of the great

Chelsea's homely feel is only enhanced by the many little stores "just round the corner", ranging from the antiques shop (above) via the book store (top right) to the hairdresser's. The Empire Diner (large picture) in 10th Avenue is a chrome-flashing art-deco jewel inside, apparently much beloved by the actress, Bette Davis.

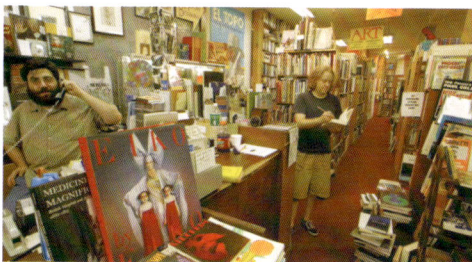

ocean liners that used to dock here. On April 16, 1912, the *Titanic*, on its maiden voyage, tragically, never reached New York. Nowadays, the area is home to a large leisure complex, with a health club, gymnast center, basketball courts, rock climbing wall, ice rinks, golf club, and dance studios.

New York is a vibrant city, continually changing and always exciting, as can be witnessed in its art. The city affords its artists more freedom and offers more inspiration than most other places in the world. However, "art needs patrons" as the Viennese composer Otto M Zykan once said. It is little wonder, perhaps, that it was in New York that pop artists such as Andy Warhol blurred the lines between artist and artisan, and former graffiti artists such as Keith Haring turned their hand to both art and merchandizing. Art in New York has to be affordable, and so many artists have had to adapt. This is especially true of female artists like Charline von Heyl, who was Jörg Immendorf's assistant and a member of Martin Kippenberger's circle; since 1996 she has been part of the New York scene, described by The *Village Voice* as revolutionary and exceptional in that she is firstly a

woman, secondly a painter, thirdly an abstract painter, and fourthly is aged over 35. While she may have a typical career, her paintings reflect New York in their vibrancy and dynamism. The recession has hit artists and art galleries hard, but there are signs that things are picking up again.

The best art galleries (above and top) are to be found in Chelsea, which styles itself the "Gallery Capital of the World". The art guide in the *New York Times* weekend supplement and the Chelsea pages in *Time Out* magazine are a good place to look for more details. There are many artists working around the galleries, such as Charline von Heyl (large picture), whose work has been called "daring, hot-blooded, and intellectual".

The Meatpacking District is on Manhattan's West Side and consists of around 20 blocks between Chelsea Market to the north and Gansevoort Street to the south. This was where butchers worked, and so the district was named; in around 1900 there were as many as 250 abattoirs and warehouses in the Meatpacking District. In the 1980s, drug dealers and prostitutes moved into the dark alleys and its reputation plummeted, a situation that only changed in the 1990s when designers, artists, and writers discovered the area. Famous fashion designers such as Diane von

Fürstenberg and Christian Louboutin, as well as companies such as Apple, opened here. They were followed by restaurants and clubs including Pastis, Buddha Bar, and Cielo. In 2009 the first section of the High Line opened, a former freight railroad modeled on the planted promenades in Paris.

The bold and the beautiful now flock to the Meatpacking District, whose dingy roads and dark alleyways (top) they would have avoided only a few years ago. There are now more upscale stores than butchers (above). If you can afford it, get an overview from the roof terrace of the Hotel The Gansevoort (large picture), while pondering by the pool what might be on offer at the "Naughty but Nice" store, below.

The lights of the big city: the two most famous Manhattan landmarks, the Chrysler and the Empire State Buildings are positioned as distinctive poles at opposite ends of this beautiful panorama of city skyscrapers.

New York's heart beats loud and fast in central Manhattan, and you can really feel the pulse of time here. Gigantic towering skyscrapers such as the Empire State, the Chrysler Building, and the Trump Tower make deep canyons of the streets. Historic buildings like Grand Central Terminal, the New York Public Library, and the United Nations Headquarters are ever-present reminders of the city's eventful history. Fifth Avenue revels in luxury, a mecca for chic shoppers and footsore tourists alike, whereas the bright neon lights of Times Square and Broadway sparkle with life both day and night in the "city that never sleeps".

"The World's Most Famous Arena" is how Madison Square Garden now advertises itself. This multi-function venue, built on Pennsylvania Plaza in 1968, is home to the New York Rangers ice hockey team and the New York Knicks basketball players; even the world-famous "Ringling Brothers and Barnum and Bailey Circus" makes guest appearance here when it visits Manhattan. Among some of the most famous events to be held at Madison Square Garden were the legendary boxing matches between Joe Frazier and Muhammad Ali, George Harrison's no less epic Concert for Bangladesh, and John Len-

non's last concert before his murder in December 1980, plus the Concert for New York City after September 11. The plain building complex contains an enormous stadium seating 20,000 people, a function room for 1,000, restaurants, malls, and there is even a cinema on the site.

The beautiful Pennsylvania Station building was demolished to make way for the complex (top), to the outrage of conservationists. Playing Madison Square Garden one day is every rock musician's and sportsman's number one dream. (large picture): a super bantam weight boxing match between Lante Addy and Jorge Diaz; (above: Kobe Bryant of the Los Angeles Lakers after playing the New York Knicks).

Since the collapse of the World Trade Center's twin towers, the Empire State is once again New York's tallest building, at 381 m (1,250 ft) in height or 449 m (1,473 ft) including the radiomast. As many as 34,000 workers, including Mohawk Native North Americans, were employed at peak times during the skyscraper's construction. Designed by the architects Schreve, Lamb & Harmon, it was opened on 1 May 1931 when President Herbert Hoover pressed a button in the White House in Washington, turning on the lights in the building. Officially there are 102 floors, but only 85 of these

The Empire State Building has been illuminated almost every night since 1975 (large picture); the lights are turned off only during the bird migration season, so the flocks do not fly into the side of the building. On public holidays the building is lit up in the national colors. Visitors are greeted by marble art deco glamour in the lobby (above). Top right: the viewing platform on the 86th floor, at 320 m (1,050 ft) high.

contain office space that can be rented. On the 86th floor of the building there is a viewing platform and at the top is a dome which was originally intended as a mooring-place for airships; this novel plan had to be abandoned, however, because of the building's dangerous updraught.

Originally called Fourth Avenue, this road had the rails of the New York and Harlem Railroad running alongside it from the 1830s – one of the first private train companies in the United States and perhaps also the first one to also operate tramways from Lower Manhattan to Harlem. In 1860 the section between 34th and 40th Streets was renamed Park Avenue (the route went through the then upscale area of Murray Hill, a green space that is at least remotely reminiscent of a "park"). Today the entire length of the street from Union Square to Harlem River Park Avenue is now Park Avenue.

The rails have long been placed underground, and the Metro North Railroad Harlem Line now runs northward from here. Above ground, between 42nd and 59th Streets, Park Avenue, has now become one of the most desirable and expensive addresses in the entire city.

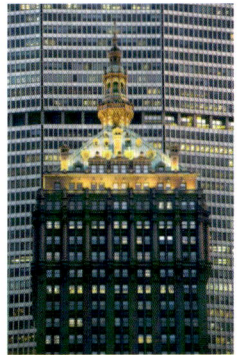

In its central section Park Avenue cuts a swathe through Midtown Manhattan (large picture), and more offices (some three million places of employment) and hotels are crowded here than in any comparable space. Some of the skyscrapers here have made architectural history. Top: the Mutual of America Building, 320 Park Avenue. Above: the Helmsley (known formerly as the New York Central) Building, 230 Park Avenue.

Built in 1930, the Chrysler Building was never intended as office space for the car firm of the same name, but instead as a lastng memorial for its owner, Walter P.Chrysler, whose career had begun on the shop floor of the Union Pacific Railroad. "His" skyscraper was to rise as steeply into the New York sky as his career had risen when he moved into the car industry, and it was not only the most beautiful but also the tallest building in the city. Most New Yorkers would agree that his architect, William Van Alen, succeeded aesthetically, and in the matter of height Van Alen found himself in a extremely bitter running battle

with his former partner, H. Craig Severance, who was now planning the tallest building in the world, not just New York, for the Bank of Manhattan Company. At 319 m (1,046 ft), the Chrysler was the victor – but this only lasted a year, after which it was overtaken by the Empire State Building.

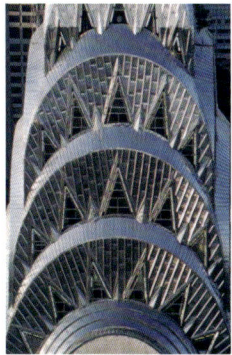

The Chrysler Building on Lexington Avenue is a masterpiece of art deco architecture: on the outside its crowning stainless-steel spire is reminiscent of the fins of a car radiator, while inside it glories in a lobby clad in chrome-plates steel. In the race to build the tallest structure in the world every trick in the book was used: thus the 55.5-m (180 ft)-long spire was secretly manufactured inside the building.

New York's skyscrapers are neither the oldest (those were built in Chicago in 1880) nor the tallest (nowadays these are all in Asia), but there are probably the most beautiful (the Chrysler Building) and the most famous (the Empire State Building). Their construction became possible with the development of resilient types of steel and safe elevators. Their load-bearing structure invariably consisted of a frame, which was generally one of two types: either a "skeleton frame" or a cantilevered frame. In the first instance, a frame mostly constructed from stable steel columns and beams supports all the walls and floors, and in the second, the main support is a central concrete column, housing the elevator and utility shafts, from which the floors are suspended. The Empire State Building was one of the last steel-framed building projects to be built with riveted steel beams before

The steel beams on which the workers had to balance were sometimes only 15 cm (6 in) across (top right). The Flatiron Building (above) is a typical steel frame building.

Large picture: From the top of a skyscraper, Henry Miller, thought you could see the soil of the old buildings on which this fantastical world of building blocks was constructed.

SKYLINE: SKY WALKERS AND SKYSCRAPERS

more reliable welded joints replaced this technique. The design and construction of New York's famous skyscrapers would have been impossible without the Mohawk ironworkers – Native American construction workers known as "skywalkers" could balance on vertiginous steel beams.

MIDTOWN MANHATTAN

The Headquarters of the United Nations (UN) is located on what is considered to be international soil on the banks of the East River, on the site of a former slaughterhouse district. John D Rockefeller Jr bought the land and donated it to the United Nations. The United States provided an interest-free loan of $67 million, and between 1947 and 1950 the plain-looking tower in which the UN Secretary-General's office is based was constructed to a design by an international committee of renowned architects that included Le Corbusier, Oscar Niemeyer, and Sven Markelius, to name but a few

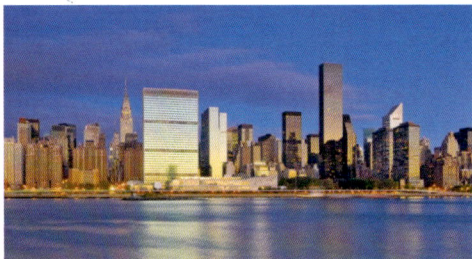

Later the General Assembly Building, which is used as an auditorium, was added, along with the Conference Building and the Dag Hamarskjöld Library. The gardens and the lobby of the General Assembly Building are open to the public and the other buildings are accessible by guided tours.

The members of the organization that followed the League of Nations (large picture: a plenary meeting; above: a conference room) have adopted common aims – the preservation of world peace and the protection of human rights. Top: the nearly 166-m-tall (545-ft) headquarters of the United Nations next to the Chrysler Building; on the right the 262-m-tall (860-ft) Trump World Tower rises into the sky.

Built in the Beaux Arts style, and decorated with baroque and Renaissance elements, Grand Central Terminal opened in its current form in 1913 after several years of construction. It remains the largest and busiest rail station in the world. A Roman triumphal arch provides an orientation point at the entrance on East 42nd Street. Corinthian columns support the giant arched windows and in the middle a bronze statue commemorates Cornelius Vanderbilt, the American railroad magnate. Known as the "Commodore", Vanderbilt combined the dozen or so railroad services he owned into the "New

York Central System" and it was his grandson who built this station. A roof decorated with stars arches over a flagstone floor in the magnificent 12-level main hall, is intended to resemble Roman baths.Referred to as Grand Central Station or just Grand Central, it is used by 125,000 commuters daily.

The station's main entrance on East 42nd Street (large picture) is adorned by three sculptures, representing Mercury, Hercules, and Minerva. The main hall (above), under a "heavenly dome", buzzes with life, and the Grand Central Oyster Bar promises "the freshest seafood in Manhattan".

New York Public Library is one of the world's greatest libraries, housing some 49.5 million documents, including more than 18 million books. It occupies a monumental Beaux Arts building located on Fifth Avenue that was designed by the architects Carrère & Hastings in 1911. Bryant Park, which adjoins the western end of the library, is also worth a visit; the HBO Bryant Park Summer Film Festival takes place here every year in June. John Pierpont Morgan (1837–1913) was not only a successful financier, but also one of the greatest collectors of rare books and original manuscripts of his time.

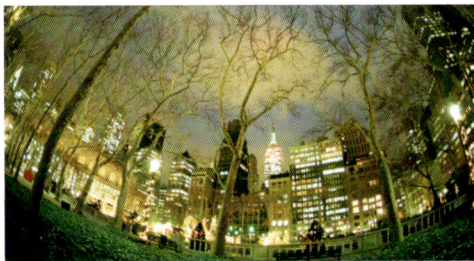

In 1906, he commissioned the architectural practice of McKim, Mead & White to design a magnificent building for the garden behind his house on Park Avenue and Madison Avenue, where his collection of treasures, including rare manuscripts, books and prints, can still be seen today.

The vast main reading room of the New York Public Library (large picture) extends across two blocks and seats some 500 readers. The adjoining Bryant Park (top) is a regular venue for open-air film screenings in summer. Among the greatest treasures in the John Pierpont Morgan collection are valuable manuscripts incunabula (above: an illustrated French bible).

Sixth Avenue runs from Little Italy in the south of Manhattan and continues to Central Park South. Although the former mayor of New York, Fiorello La Guardia, renamed it Avenue of the Americas in 1945, the new name never quite caught on, and the street signs have carried both names since the 1980s. The avenue is also known as Fashion Road due to the many department stores that were located here between 14th Street and Herald Square around the end of the 19th century. One of the original stores, Macy's, is still thriving today. The elevated tracks of the Sixth Avenue Line

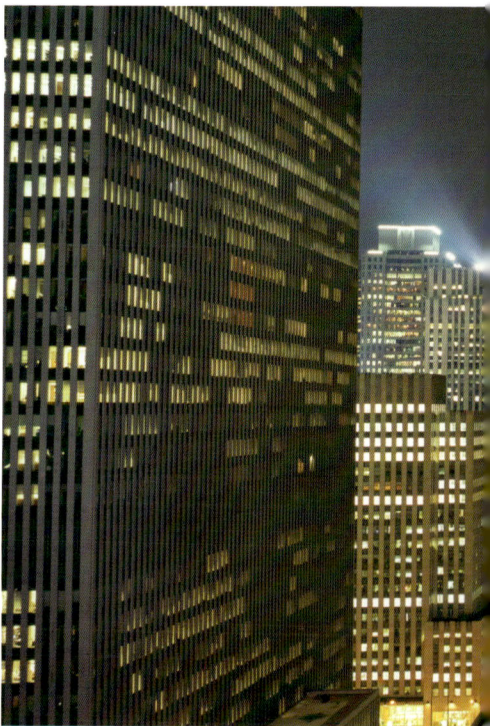

Glazed tower blocks abound, and nothing remains of the period around the turn of the 19th to the 20th centuries, when the ladies of New York's upper classes drove to Broadway in their horse-drawn carts to shop at the elegant department stores of "Ladies Mile" between 18th and 23rd Streets. The middle classes did their shopping at the same level in the "Fashion Road" section of Sixth Avenue, in the shadow of the elevated railroad.

used to overshadow the road until 1939. When the railway was closed down and replaced by the IND Sixth Avenue Subway, office blocks shot up, including the CBS Building, the 38-floor headquarters of the media concern, also known as Black Rock because of its granite cladding.

Broadway is one of the most famous street in the whole world. It was originally the Algonquin Native North American warpath and today is also known as "The Great White Way" due to its many bright lights. It's a microcosm to which the rock journalist and travel writer Nik Cohn (whose reports had created the starting point for the film *Saturday Night Fever*) dedicated his entire book, which he called *The Heart of the World*. Inspiration for his book was easy to find on Broadway: he just had to go there. And that's still the best way to explore Broadway, which has long since become a

legendary name. The road runs diagonally across the checkerboard grid, from Bowling Green in Downtown through Manhattan and far beyond to the Bronx. The most famous section of Broadway can be found mainly between 41st and 53rd Street, where you'll also find Times Square.

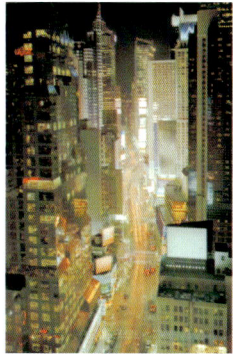

Originally Nik Cohn planned a voyage around the world. But then he recognized: " if you walked a block along Broadway and opened all the doors, you would discover a hundred different worlds." And so he set off on his personal journey …

If showbusiness has a birth place, it must be found in New York. Even during the initial waves of immigration, theater performances were considered a very welcome escape from the trials of the immigrants' daily lives. The theatre was almost a second home for them not least because many of the plays were performed in their mother tongues. Initially there were only amateur performances; the first professional production was of Shakespeare's *Richard III* at the New Theater in Nassau Street in 1750. The 19th century was the great era of vaudeville shows, which combined drama, music, comedy, and circus acts. The start of the 20th century saw the dawning of the real age of Broadway, as more theaters opened in the area around Times Square, the center of New York night life at the time. The Empire Theater moved from Herald Square to Broadway in 1893, and from then

SHOWTIME: LIVE ON BROADWAY

until 1930 many theaters opened, such as the New Lyceum. After a crisis in the 1980s, musicals such as *Cats*, *The Phantom of the Opera*, and *The Lion King* continued the earlier successes. Nowadays, there are still around 40 major theaters on Broadway and a multitude of smaller ones.

Although Broadway crosses the whole of Manhattan from north to south, its worldwide fame originated mainly in the so-called "Theater District" north of Times Square, with its many musicals, theatrical performances, and shows advertised by bright billboards. In part, Broadway follows the route of a Native American trail, which was taken over by the first Dutch settlers and enlarged to become a "broad way".

You can hear New York's heart-beat on Times Square. The city fleshpots of yesteryear have become a Disney-style consumer arena. Mighty shopping malls and themed restaurants now set the tone in a place which once was notorious for its seamy side: the pickpockets, drug dealers, and hookers have moved on and the XXX-rated posters, porn stores, and peep-shows are now all but forgotten. In 1900 the Square was still a rural community called Longacre Square and was a storage area with barns and stables for horses. It was re-named Times Square in 1904, in honor of the New

York Times, newspaper which was building a giant office block there. Events from all over the world have flashed across the news screens on the façade since 1928; nowadays, the *Times* is edited from 43rd Street. Each year crowds congregate in the square for the New Year celebrations.

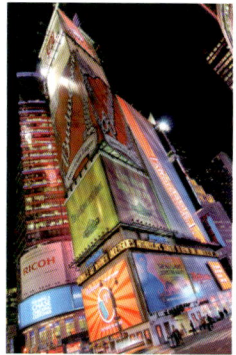

The New York building code prescribes that all new builds on Times Square are to be fitted with brightly lit advertising hoardings, to maintain its current, well-known appearance. Some landlords earn more from the advertising signs than they ever could in rent. In May 2009 Times Square was transformed into a pedestrian-only zone – with the exception of 7th Avenue, the only street that is still entirely open to traffic.

Dividing Manhattan's Streets into East and West, Fifth Avenue begins at Washington Square in Greenwich Village, crosses Midtown, passes Central Park, and runs along the Upper East Side to the Harlem River. In the second half of the 19th century, well-off families – the Astors, Forbes, Fricks, Rockefellers, Vanderbilts, and others – were looking for ways to escape cramped southern Manhattan. They built their villas along Fifth Avenue's first few miles, giving it the nickname of "Millionaires' Row". By the beginning of the 20th century more and more businesses were

moving in, causing the super rich – who today mostly live around Central Park – to venture further uptown. There are now flagship stores belonging to famous brands, such as Prada Armani, Cartier, Chanel, and Versace, to draw the crowds, and you might even go to have *Breakfast at Tiffany's* …

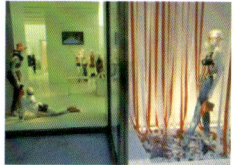

You'll find upmarket goods on Fifth Avenue, which runs north-south through the deep gorges created by the skyscrapers in Manhattan (top): people usually refer to the stretch between 48th and 59th Streets when they speak of Fifth Avenue – thus is where the most expensive and luxurious stores are concentrated (above). The trendy Apple Store (767 Fifth Avenue, large picture) is open 365 days a year and 24/7.

New York is shopping heaven. Macy's, for example, the biggest department store in the world, is split between two buildings and has a sales floor of no less than 200,000 sq. m (2.1 million sq ft), spread over ten floors. Bloomingdale's sells smart designer fashion at – sometimes –reasonably afford- able prices, while Lord & Taylor's in the Empire State Building has classic upmarket styles. Diamond Row, between 40th and 50th Streets, is so called for the glittering jewels on display. Among the most popular stores on Fifth Avenue are Tiffany & Co., Prada, Versace, and FAO Schwarz, toy heaven, and not just for children. Antiques, art, and fashion are found in the "scene" districts of SoHo and TriBeCa, and Greenwich Village is famous for its weird and alternative stores, which are ideal for books, records, CDs, and esoteric odds and ends; there are also specialist shops for the

ALL THAT MONEY CAN BUY: SHOPPING IN NEW YORK

gay scene. Discount stores have congregated on Herald Square, in the shadow of Macy's, and you can buy reasonably priced fashion, bags, and shoes on historic Orchard Street in the East Village. You really can shop till you drop as there is something new and exciting around every corner.

Sisley's striking store windows stand out and draw you in (large picture), Macy's (top), and Victoria's Secret (above) on Fifth Avenue. Faced with such a wide choice, it's no wonder so many visitors to New York succumb to shopping fever, but it's also worth bearing in mind that goods of a value of no more than $800 can be imported tax free into the European Union.

The Trump Tower on the corner of Fifth Avenue and 56th Street is not beautiful, but it is worh a visit. Built to the design of Der Scutt of the architectural office of Swanke, Hayden Connell and officially completed on November 30, 1983, the 202-m-tall (663-ft) 68-floor glass palace stands as a symbol to the rise of the real estate tycoon Donald Trump, who created an urban monument for himself with this tower. The Trump International Hotel and Tower in Central Park had opened as early as 1971, and in 2001 the Trump World Tower near the United Nations Head-quarters was added to his New

The main attraction in the Trump Tower (above: view from Fifth Avenue; top right: one of the live-ried employees at the entrance) is the six-floor tall atrium (large picture), whose walls and floors were built in Italian marble – its combination of pink, peach, and orange hues harmonize beauti-fully with the golden escalators. The "waterfall" turns out to be not much more than a trickle, but it does provide a gentle splashing sound while you're shopping.

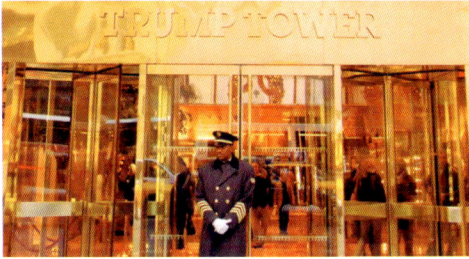

York portfolio, but none of these buildings made "The Donald" as popular as the Trump Tower. The entrance lobby of the famous building on Fifth Avenue is lavishly adorned by two free-standing golden Ts, and plenty of gold and silver also set the scene for the interior of the glass palace.

Designed by Schultze & Weaver, this legendary hotel on Park Avenue opened for business in 1931 and is still one of the city's most fascinating art deco buildings. Cole Porter's piano stands in the lobby, and it is still being played today. "Waldorf=Astoria" is officially written with two dashes, as it had originally been two hotels linked by a connecting corridor. "*Meet me at The Hyphen*" became a popular song and expression at the time, with the "hyphen" used to refer to the hotel, but the name did not stick. William Waldorf Astor built the first 13-floor Waldorf Hotel here in 1893, and four years later his

When the Waldorf-Astoria (top right: the entrance lobby) was opened on 1 October 1931 it was the biggest hotel in the world. There is a large clock in the lobby (large picture) which was originally made for the World's Fair in Chicago in 1893; it already adorned the first Waldorf Hotel.

cousin, John Jacob Astor, built the Astoria, which was four floors higher, right next door. The upheaval of construction work on the Empire State Building meant that the hotels had to close during that period. When the new hotel was built, the name was changed to Waldorf-Astoria.

The Citigroup Center (formerly Citicorp Center) was designed by Hugh Stubbins & Associates – now called KlingStubbins – and built in 1977 on four nine-floor stilts. The stilts were not placed at the corners of the rectangular building, but were instead situated in the middle of each side. This was because trustees of St Peter's Church would only sell part of their land and property rights on the sole condition that they would be allowed to construct a new church "under" the skyscraper. This now stands beneath the extended north-west corner of the Citigroup Center. Opposite stands the "Lipstipck Building"

designed by John Burgee in 1986 and completed by Philip Johnson. The Sony Building located on Madison Avenue was built in 1984 for AT&T, and is now called the Sony Tower. Designed by Philip Johnson, his design for the "world's first post-modern skyscraper" continues to cause controversy.

Solar panels were originally planned to be installed on the oblique top of the Citigroup Centers (large picture, but this proved impossible. The Sony Building (above) is also called "Chippendale", because the block's gable end is reminiscent of furniture of that name. With its elliptical ground plan, the skyscraper known officially by its address as 53rd at Third, resembles lipstick (top, on the right in the picture).

One of New York City's most successful art deco creations is this strikingly beautiful building on 570 Lexington Avenue. Originally built in 1931 to a design by the Cross & Cross practice for the broadcasters RCA ("Radio Corporation of America"), it later became the headquarters of the General Electric power company. The historic building – not to be confused with the GE (General Electric) Building, which is in the Rockefeller Center – makes an interesting architectural reference to St Bartholomew's Church, which stands beside it. When the General Electric office block was constructed,

the materials used – stone, brick and aluminium– were chosen to harmonize with the church, which had been built from the same materials. The rear elevation of the General Electric building, was styled partly to form a backdrop to the church. The architectural harmony is visually stunning.

The General Electric Building's art deco crown (large picture and top) suggests radio waves, after the broadcasting company, which commissioned the building. When the company moved into the Rockefeller Center in 1931, it was renamed from the original RCA Victor Building as the General Electric Building. The lobby also has art deco features, and the clock (above) boasts a GE monogram for "General Electric".

In 1828 the Roman Catholic Church in New York bought a parcel of landoutside the city limits for use as a cemetery. In 1850, after the undersoil had proved too stony for that purpose, Archbishop John Hughes decided to commission a European-style cathedral along lines for this spot on Fifth Avenue. Eight years later work on a neo-Gothic cathedral designed by the architect James Renwick started; it was completed in 1879. Her spires were built in 1888 and The Lady Chapel in 1906. In 1910 it was dedicated to St Patrick, the patron saint of Ireland. A statue within its walls com-

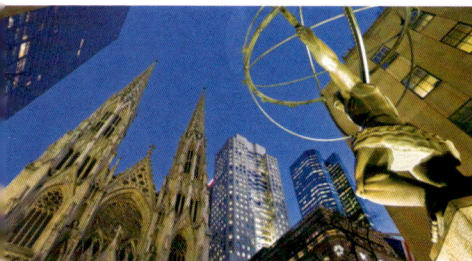

memorates Elizabeth Ann Seton (1774–1821), the founder of the order of the Sisters of Charity and the first American citizen to be canonized. St Patrick's Cathedral, which can hold 2,500, is the seat of the archbishop of New York. Over 5 million people per year come to the cathedral to visit or pray.

Atlas may carry the world, but the clergy provide the spiritual leadership (top). The two 101-m (331-ft) high towers were added only nine years after the completion of the church, which was constructed to last – the massive bronze doors (above) alone weigh 9 tons (8,000 m). Inside, the vault is supported by mighty marble columns (large picture).

New York 113

MIDTOWN MANHATTAN

This gigantic complex of sky-scrapers located between 47th and 50th Streets was built in the 1930s for John D Rockefeller Jr by a team of architects led by Raymond Hood. The complex has since been extended several times and houses offices, television studios, restaurants, and stores. Built in 1933 to a height of 260 m (853 ft), the GE (General Electric) Building is at the heart of the complex. From its viewing platform, known as "Top of the Rocks", you can enjoy some stunning views of the city's skyline. The GE Building is also home to the broadcaster NBC, whose legendary *Today* show

– the oldest factual television show, first screened on 14 January 1952 – is broadcast every morning from 7.00 till 9.00 from a studio in the GE Building. Less well known is the underground concourse, home to stores, fast food outlets and other venues, New York's largest underground city.

Paul Manship's statue of Prometheus (top) guards the Rockefeller Plaza (right), the heart of the Rockefeller Center. In winter it is transformed into an ice rink. The Rockefeller Center is the largest such complex in private ownership. The central building is the GE (General Electric) Building (large picture). The statue of Atlas (above) in front of the International Building was created by Lee Lawrie and Renee Paul Chambellan in 1937.

Descended from a family that emigrated to New York from a small German hamlet to the New World in the 18th century, John Davison Rockefeller Sr (1839–1937) worked himself up from his humble beginnings to become head of an oil dynasty whose influence can still be felt to this day. His father, William, had traveled door to door as a quack doctor to feed his family of eight, and at 16 John began an apprenticeship with a haulage company where he heled to keep the books. At the age of 19 he moved into the oil business, founding the "Standard Oil Company" (a direct forerunner of today's Exxon Mobil Corporation) in 1870 and the "Standard Oil Trust" in 1882. Soon they controlled more than ninety percent of the refinery capacity of the entire United States. Determined to secure his monopoly with every means possible, Rockefeller's occasionally roughshod busi-

ROCKEFELLER: OIL MAGNATE AND PHILANTHROPIST

ness tactics provoked legislation in 1890 (the Sherman Antitrust Act), which in 1911 saw his business broken up into separate companies. To improve his reputation, he endowed many charitable trusts, such as the Rockefeller Foundation to which he donated more than $500 million.

Like father, like son: the company founder's sole male heir, John Davison Rockefeller Jr (1874–1960), also showed entrepreneurial spirit. Disregarding the global financial crisis of the 1930s he built the Rockefeller Center (large picture: the Rockefeller Plaza). He can be seen as a "construction worker" (top left) on the site of the Rockefeller Center in 1939, at the opening of Radio City Music Hall 1932, and above with his father in 1915.

Art deco is a term describing one of the most imaginative, whimsical, and artistic movements of the 1920s and 1930s. The name originally came from a crafts exhibition (the "Exposition Internationale des Arts Decoratifs et Industriels Modernes") that was held in Paris in 1925 and soon attracted interest across the Atlantic. Emerging from the art nouveau style, it influenced every branch of art and design, as well as fashion, furniture, and architecture. The designs were typified by an apparent contradiction between grace and strength, which created contrapuntal accents as in music. The geometric shapes are usually strict and formal, whereas the lavish decorations are mostly graceful. For the ornamentation the artists used smooth, precious surfaces made from marble and granite, steel, chrome and Bakelite – often in daring combinations of different hues. In the e boom

ART DÉCO: DECORATIVE AND WHIMSICAL

years of early high-rise construction, art deco offered New York's architects all kinds possibilities: artistic decoration outshone mere functionality, streamlining the skyscrapers' block-like appearance and bringing a playful element to the city's otherwise rather sober building styles.

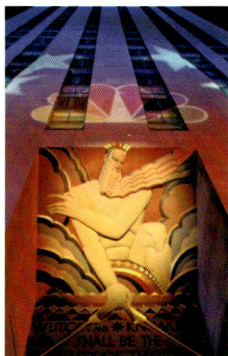

Among New York's art deco gems are the monumental Rockefeller Center, where works by 30 artists can be admired in the foyers and gardens and on the façades. Above: Lee Lawrie's *Wisdom* relief at the main entrance of the GE Building; large picture: *The Joy of Life*, by Attillo Piccirilli (1937, 1 Rockefeller Plaza); top: *Dance, Drama, and Song*, by Hildreth M Meiere (1932, Radio City Music Hall).

Radio City Music Hall, which is also part of the Rockefeller Center, has gone down in history as the "showplace of the nation". Designed by the architect Edward Durell for the impresario Samuel "Roxy" Rothafel, who had found fame and fortune during the silent film era, the complex was officially opened on 27 December 1932 and has since had more than 300 million visitors from around the world. Originally intended as a variety hall, the 6,200-seat auditorium was refurbished as a cinema that could also host stage productions. The dance troupe, the Rockettes, became legendary,

Just before the millennium, Radio City Music Hall, which is a listed national monument, underwent the most extensive renovation in its history: over $70 million was spent in creating the most up-to-date technology whilst retaining its historic ambience.

and took part in the traditional annual Christmas shows that began in 1933. Nowadays, Radio City Music Hall is best known as alive venue for rock stars. The remaining Beatles, Paul McCartney and Ringo Starr, took part in a charity concert for the David Lynch Foundation on 4 April 2009.

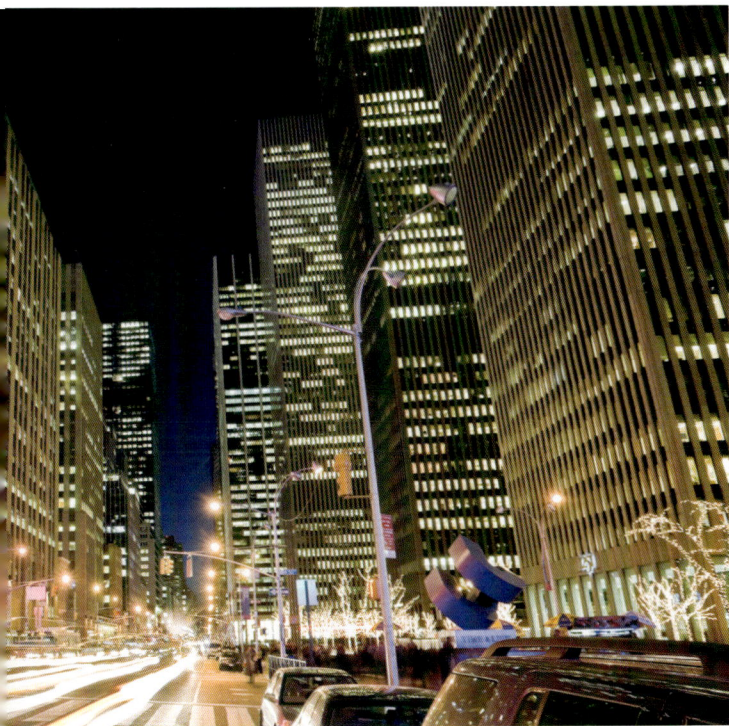

Originally made famous by Liza Minnelli and Frank Sinatra, *New York, New York*, became the city's soundtrack and motto. Composed by Fred Ebb and John Kander *Theme from New York, New York*, the song's full name, is the title song of the musical film with the same name, which was screened in the cinemas in 1977 and was nominated for four Golden Globes. Liza Minnelli and Robert De Niro played the leads, and Martin Scorsese directed. The film tells the story of a musician and a singer, who get married after World War II and need to sacrifice their love in order to further their careers. At the end of the film Liza Minnelli sings *New York, New York*, a passionate declaration of love for the big city. Liza Minnelli and Frank Sinatra both included the song in their regular concert programs and stylized it as a hymn. In March 1980 Sinatra released the song as a single, and there are several live recordings by both artists. This song is often

Francis Albert Sinatra (1915–1998; top right: with Count Basie) was born in Hoboken (New Jersey), the son of Italian immigrants. He sang in the big bands of Harry James and Tommy Dorsey, gaining the epithet of "the voice" in the process, and collected numerous hits that always guaranteed him a full house (above and large picture). Sinatra's interpretation of *My Way*, is a musical classic.

FRANK SINATRA: "NEW YORK, NEW YORK"

confused, however, with another song also entitled *New York, New York* and written by Leonard Bernstein, Betty Comden, and Adolph Green, from the 1944 musical *On the Town*, and also sung by Frank Sinatra. This beautiful outpouring of love for the metropolis became an anthem in its own right.

All it took was three good friends. In a clear case of girl power, the Museum of Modern Art (MoMA) was founded in 1929 by Mary Quinn Sullivan, Abby Aldrich Rockefeller, and Lillie P Bliss, although the museum's official history still doggedly refers to the first two as Mrs Cornelius J Sullivan and Mrs John D Rockefeller, Jr – only Lillie, who never married, is credited under her own first name. All three were proven patrons of the arts (and artists) and decided to find a common home for their passion and for their collections. The ladies enlisted art historian Alfred H Barr as its founding director

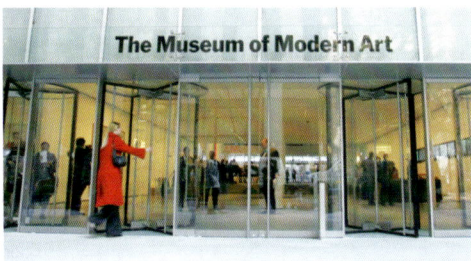

and he introduced the MoMA'S multi-departmental structure. It moved location several times before ending up at its current site, built to a design by the architects Philip Goodwin and Edward Durell in 1939. Its rich, diverse content make it one of the world's most comprehensive art collections.

Right from the start the MoMA was laid out as "the greatest museum of modern art in the world" (Alfred H Barr Jr). The comprehensive collection also includes Claude Monet's *Waterlilies* (c. 1920), which extends over 12 m (39 ft) (large picture). Between 2002 and 2004 the space for exhibitions and other activities of the museum was nearly doubled to around 58,000 sq m (624,080 sq ft).

Fifth Avenue comes to a fitting end at Grand Army Plaza by Central Park, at whose southeast entrance horse-drawn buggies begin their pleasure trips through the park. Built in 1915, the Pulitzer fountain which is in the middle commemorates the famous publisher, and the Plaza's northern half boasts an equestrian statue of William Tecumseh Sherman, the Civil War General. Built by Henry J. Hardenberg in 1907 in the style of a French chateau, the legendary Plaza hotel was once advertised with the slogan "Nothing boring ever happens at the Plaza". Some $400 million was spent on restorati-

A night in the Plaza Hotel (top right: with the equestrian statue of the Civil War General Willliam Tecumseh Sherman in the foreground; above: the entrance area) at the harmoniously designed Grand Army Plaza is affordable to few; many, however, can enjoy an afternoon tea in the famous Palm Court. Large picture: the wealthy celebrate their own good fortunes at the debutantes' ball – and also donate a lot of money to charities.

ons between 2005 and 2007, and the slogan still applies. Today the site is no longer "just" a hotel – some of the area is now turned over to private homes, with stores, bars, and restaurants that are open to the public. The Plaza has been awarded national historic landmark status.

Perhaps it was a good omen that the architect William B. Tuthill not only had a passion for music, but also played the cello, since Carnegie Hall, built to his design between 1890 and 1891 for the millionaire steel magnate Andrew Carnegie, remains one of the world's most renowned concert halls.

As well as its magnificent architecture, it is celebrated for its fantastic acoustics. They were first acclaimed in May 1891, when the Hall was opened with a five-day festival featuring, among others, the Russian composer Peter Tchaikovsky as a guest conductor. It has since been the venue for

Carnegie Hall (above and large picture the entrance lobby; top right: the Isaac Stern Auditorium) was the home of the New York Philharmonic for many years, with Arturo Toscanini, Bruno Walter, and Leonard Bernstein among its famous conductors. When the Philharmonic moved to the Lincoln Center, the hall was faced with demolition, eliciting worldwide protests, which fortunately saved the venue.

important jazz events, historic lectures, educational forums, as well as many concerts. Carnegie Hall consists of three concert halls, namely the Isaac Stern Auditorium (seating 2,800), the Joan and Sanford I Weill Recital Hall (seating 268), and the Judy and Arthur Zankel Hall (seating 599).

Midtown's north-western tip is formed by Columbus Circle, a roundabout that forms the gateway to the Upper West Side. In the middle of the roundabout there is a statue of Columbus by Gaetano Russo, which was erected in 1892 to commemorate the 400th anniversary of the "discovery" of America. The statue is also the reference point for the measurement of all distances to and from New York City. The angular glass building of the Time Warner Center, a major landmark built in 2004 to a design by the architect David Childs, continues the traditions of the twin towers built on the west

However much the traffic rumbles around the square, Columbus remains unmoved (top right), and no wonder – he's made of marble and was a gift to New York City from the Italian-American community. The square is dominated by the 229-m (751-ft) high twin towers of the Time Warner Center (above and large picture).

side of Central Park. Situated inside the complex, which cost $1.8 billion to build, are the headquarters of Time Warner Inc., after whom it is named, CNN's studios, luxury apartments, a Mandarin Oriental Hotel, as well as a number of restaurants, several stores, and a whole food market.

The true extent of Central Park only becomes apparent when it is seen from the air. Upper East Side (in the foreground) once known as the "Silk Stocking District", is one of the most affluent areas in New York City.

CENTRAL PARK AND UPPER EAST SIDE

North of 59th Street, Central Park divides Manhattan into the Upper East Side and the Upper West Side. The park is a green oasis in the centre of the urban mass, a space where you can jog, boat, rock-climb, or just relax. People who live right by Park can count their blessings: a view that enjoys green space rather than buildings is virtually unaffordable in New York. Madonna's townhouse located on the Upper East Side is said to have changed hands for a cool $40 million. Running along the eastern edge of Central Park, Fifth Avenue then turns into the famous "Museum Mile" with some of the best museums in the world.

Construction began on Central Park in north Manhattan in 1858, realizing a lifelong dream for American landscape architect Frederick Law Olmsted and his partner, British-born Calvert Vaux. Together they created a "green lung" in the ever-expanding city, which today extends from 59th to 110th Street and covers a vast 340 ha (1,016 acres), representing six percent of Manhattan's total area. It became the second-largest park in the city after Jamaica Bay Park in Queens (1,150 ha/3,440 acres). Free open-air concerts are held here in the summer and information on these stage

performances and other events in the park can be found at the Visitors' Center, located in a neo-Gothic building designed by Olmsted and Vaux called The Dairy. Or you simply stroll into this wonderful green area and while away the day in the lovely park, relaxing and enjoying the fresh air.

Designed by man rather than nature, the result is nonetheless quite beautiful: many million truckloads of earth and stones had to be carted here, and more than 500,000 trees and shrubs were planted in order to transform the once marshy terrain into a recreation area. On Sundays the park becomes an open-air stage for New Yorkers.

Before you spend time in the museums close to Central Park, enjoy a visit to one of New York's most celebrated temples. Bloomingdale's is further east on the Upper East Side. and one of Manhattan's most cherished landmarks. An entire block between East 59th and 60th Streets as well as Lexing- ton and Third Avenue has been transformed into a consumers' paradise where you can browse and shop as much as your heart desires. Built in 1930 to designs by the archi- tects Starrett & Van Vleck, the New York headquarters of the department store chain which was founded in 1860 by the

brothers Joseph and Lyman Bloomingdale, carries everything, from furniture and clothes to housewares – all of it of the finest quality and often at more reasonable prices than you'd expect. With a vast range of goods to choose from, a visit to Bloomingdale's can be a day out in itself.

The lavish shop window decorations at Bloomingdale's are legendary in their own right, not only at Christmas, but throughout the year. The displays are beautifully designed and illustrate the ingenuity of the "visual merchandizers" who create windows which reflect the wealth of goods on offer at the great department store.

In 1905, Pittsburgh steel magnate Henry Clay Frick (1849–1919) and his wife moved to New York to live out their twilight years. An avid art collector, Frick spent $5 million building an imposing French neo-classical townhouse on the corner of Fifth Avenue and 70th Street to a design by Carrère & Hastings; it was to become a very worthy setting for his great collection. Frick later bequeathed the house, which covers a full city block, and its valuable contents to the nation and in 1935, after the death of his widow, Adelaide Frick, it was turned into a museum that is now one of the

When Henry Clay Frick saw the residence of his fiercest rival, Andrew Carnegie, in "Millionaires' Row" on the Upper East Side, he decided to have a villa built so grand (large picture: including an organ on the stairs), that he'd "make that house look like a miner's shack!". Among the work of art that can today be seen in the museum are works by Jean-Honoré Fragonard (above) and Georges de La Tour (top).

best small art museums in the country. The museum houses a collection of Old Masters, as well as French furniture, enamel work from Limoges and Italian Renaissance bronzes. Highlights include Holbein the Younger's beautiful *Portrait of Sir Thomas More* and *The Polish Rider* by Rembrandt.

In 1918, Gertrude Vanderbilt Whitney (1875–1942), a highly respected sculptor in her own right, opened an art gallery in her studio in Greenwich Village. She concentrated on American contemporary art and by the end of the 1920s had amassed a collection of about 700 canvases and sculptures, which she intended to donate to the Metropolitan Museum of Art. Her gift was refused, however, because the museum was more interested in European art, and so in 1931 she founded the Whitney Museum of American Art, which is now considered one of the most significant collections of 20th-

and 21st-century American art. All the big names – including Edward Hopper, Jasper Johns, Roy Lichtenstein, and Andy Warhol – are represented here. There are also plans to design and build a 18,116-sq m (195,000-sq ft) Witney Museum in the Meatpacking district in downtown Manhattan.

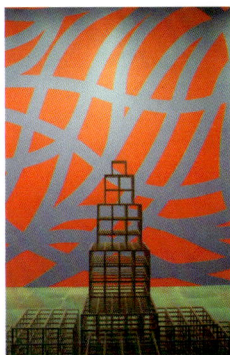

The Museum showcases contemporary American art, whether in solo exhibitions such as this one dedicated to Sol LeWitt (above and large picture) or within the framework of the Whitney Biennial of American Art that has been taking place here since 1932. The museum was built to the designs of Bauhaus student Marcel Breuer in 1966 (top) and is supposed to evoke an upside-down pyramid.

In common with the British Museum in London, the Louvre in Paris, and the Hermitage in St Petersburg, the Metropolitan Museum of Modern Art, known as the "Met" for short, is one of the greatest museums in the world. It was founded by wealthy New Yorkers and leading artists of the day who wanted to make art accessible to the people. Designed by Calvert Vaux and Jacob Wrey Mould, and expanded several times since its construction in 1870, it houses more than two million exhibits from five millennia of art history. The collection is arranged both geographically and chronologically.

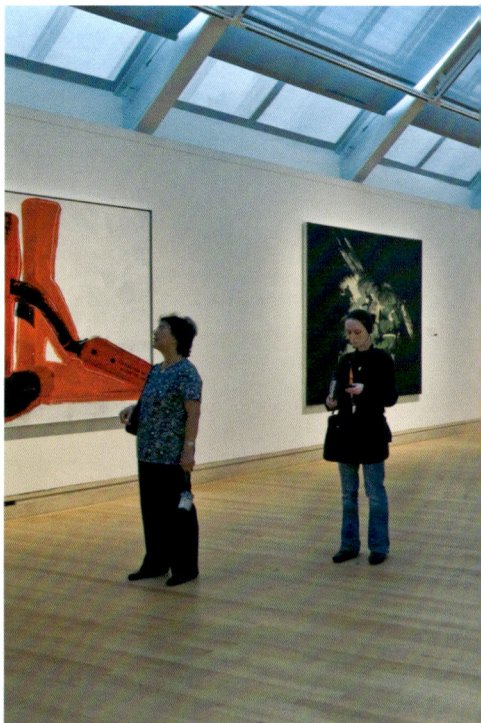

The museum welcomes more than five million visitors a year (above: a statue by Randolph Rogers depicting the blind flower girl of Pompeii; large picture: one of the exhibition rooms; top right: a house by Roy Liechtenstein on the roof terrace). During the inauguration of the new American Wing in May 2009, Michelle Obama revealed that she and her husband had their first date in a museum.

First-time visitors are often overwhelmed by the museum's sheer scope – where else can you see an Egyptian temple, a Rembrandt self-portrait, and Frank Lloyd Wright's studio under the same roof? The Met also has a sculpture garden on its roof terrace, with a fantastic view of the Manhattan skyline.

Neither Frank Lloyd Wright, the architect who designed the museum's original building, nor Solomon R Guggenheim, the coal and steel industrialist who commissioned it, lived to see this iconic gallery's inauguration in 1959. They were thus spared the initially scathing criticism the museum attracted: John Canaday, the art critic of the New York Times, is recorded as saying: "The Solomon R Guggenheim Museum is a war between architecture and painting in which both come out badly maimed". Resembling an inverted snail shell from the outside, the

building took 16 years to complete. Lit from above by a glass skylight, a central spiral ramp runs through the interior from the main level to the top of the building, along which you can admire the paintings. The building is today considered an architectural icon of its age.

Modern circles: Frank Lloyd Wright's building, which holds the important collection of abstract paintings owned by millionaire Solomon R Guggenheim, is impressive both inside and out. A ramp with a five-percent incline winds its way around the 28.5-m-tall (93.5-ft) internal rotunda five times.

Elegant apartment blocks line the park: the twin towers of the Majestic Apartments (on the left) and the San Remo Apartments (on the right) frame two smaller, neighbors – the Dakota and the Langham Buildings.

A district principally inhabited by well-off New Yorkers, much like its counterpart on the East Side, the Upper West Side is an upscale area, bounded by Central Park, the Hudson River, 59th, and 125th Streets. West of Harlem, which has become an ever more attractive bastion of black consciousness, and not just since the election of Barrack Obama as the U.S. President, you'll find Columbia University in Morningside Heights, known as the "Acropolis of the academic". Further north you'll be surprised by Manhattan's medieval (yes, indeed!) estates – the remaining architectural fragments of European monasteries known as The Cloisters.

Situated on Columbus and Amsterdam Avenues between 62nd and 66th Streets, The Lincoln Center for the Performing Arts is a cultural complex housing the Metropolitan Opera, the New York City Ballet, and the New York Philharmonic Orchestra, among others. Planned on the initiative of a group of civic leaders, including John D. Rockefeller III, most of the complex was built in the 1960s under the direction of the architect Wallace K. Harrison. The chosen site was a former slum area called "San Juan Hill"; it had been the scene of fights between rival street gangs that inspired Leonard

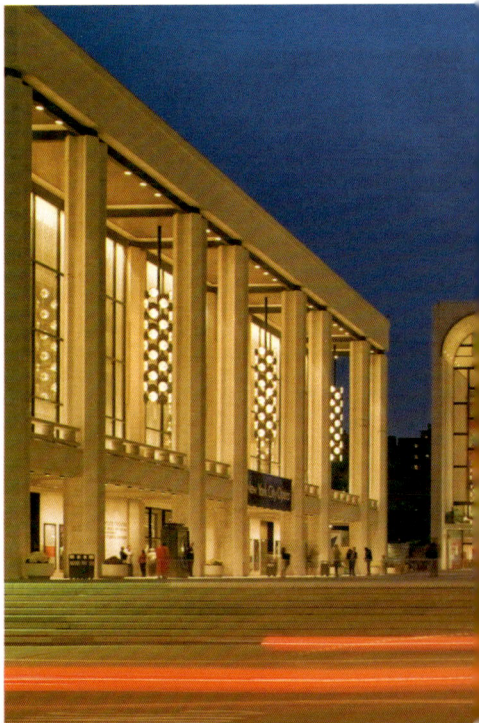

Large picture: the Metropolitan Opera House is located in the middle of the cultural center, next to the David H Koch Theater (left) and the Avery Fisher Hall (right), home of the New Yorker Philharmonic. Leonard Bernstein, successful as a pianist as well as a composer and conductor (top right), directed the orchestra for eleven years, from 1958 to 1969.

LINCOLN CENTER FOR THE PERFORMING ARTS 58

Bernstein to write the musical *West Side Story*, filmed in 1961. The complex forms part of the series of renovations designed to improve conditions in this otherwise infamous part of the Upper West Side, but more than 7,000 families and 800 businesses were displaced by the development.

The "Met" is one of the world's greatest opera houses – singing here is like qualifying for the opera equivalent of Mount Olympus. The façade of the opera house, built to a design by Wallace K Harrison and inaugurated in 1966, also has an Olympic feel. Five strikingly high arched windows allow a view into the foyer where two murals by Marc Chagall, both some 10 m (33 ft) square, proclaim the origins and triumphs of music. With an estimated value of $20 million, these paintings are not only beautiful, but also collateral for a loan that the Met was forced to take out in the spring

of 2009 as a result of the credit crunch. The original opera house, the Old Met, where Caruso and Callas once sang, was on Broadway. It opened in 1883 with a performance of *Faust*, but was demolished in 1967. Today opera perfrmances are beamed live into cinemas around the world.

The Met can seat an audience of 3,800 (top), who can enjoy lavishly staged opera productions such as Wagner's *Rheingold* (large picture) or the most artistic ballets (above: a scene from Yuri Grigorovich's *Spartacus*).

Founded on 6 April 1869, construction work on the monumental Roman triumphal building of the American Museum of Natural History began in 1874 to a design by Calvert Vaux and Jacob Wrey Mould. The museum was officially opened in 1877 and is one of the oldest and largest natural history museums in the world, with 35 million specimens, only a small percentage of which can be displayed at any one time. The museum consists of 15 buildings that are interconnected, housing its many exhibition halls and research laboratories. Here you can gain a profound insight into the his-

The American Museum of Natural History is only open in the daytime. However, the films starring Ben Stiller as a night watchman show what can happen during a *Night at the Museum*. Exhibits such as the gigantic dinosaur skeletons (large picture) can fire the imagination during the day as well. Inspiration is also available at the 40-m-high (131-ft) Rose Center for Earth and Space (above).

tory of our world and of space. Worth seeing are the dinosaur skeletons, a life-size replica blue whale, and a 19-m (63-ft) long Haida Native North American canoe. The Rose Center has extended the exhibition space by a quarter. A brilliant glass cube, it also houses the Hayden Planetarium.

"Think big": when the Cathedral of St John the Divine on 112th Street is completed, it might go down in the history of sacred architecture as the largest cathedral in the world. Begun in a Byzantine-Romanesque style by Heins & La Farge, the foundation stone was laid on 27 December 1892. Although a neo-Gothic extension was added by Cram & Ferguson in 1911, even today this church is only two-thirds finished. Both construction, and now also renovation, are an ongoing process. With 20,000 students, Columbia University, founded in 1754 as King's College and later re-

Alma Mater, the "nourishing mother", guards Columbia University's Low Library (top right), whose main entrance is located in 116th Street. The Cathedral of St John the Divine (above and large picture) is a great unfinished project: After the attacks on Pearl Harbor in 1941 construction was stopped and wasn't resumed until 1978. In 2001 a fire prevented a continuation of the work – the necessary renovation took until 2008.

named, is one of the oldest, largest, and, with Harvard, Princeton, and Yale, one of the most respected universities in the country. Its faculties of law, medicine, and journalism are renowned and today the Ivy League university can boast more than 50 Nobel Prize-winners amongst its graduates.

The Cloisters is a museum of medieval art of a kind unique in the United States. Its central building incorporates fragments from cloisters and other medieval buildings that were collected in Europe by the sculptor George Gray Barnard, and then assembled and expanded into a museum by the architects Allen, Collins & Willis in the 1930s. Thanks to the financial support of John D. Rockefeller Jr, the museum, located high above the Hudson River in Fort Tyron Park in the wooded north of Manhattan, has been a branch of the Metropolitan Museum of Modern Art since 1925. Its

Exhibits of an entire epoch were transplanted from continent to continent and today visitors can see the development of architecture in the Middle Ages between the 12th and the 15th centuries. The museum includes not only parts of cloisters, abbeys, and chapels (above and largepicture) but also medieval works of art, such as these busts from an altar made in Baden-Württemberg, Germany around 1470 (top right).

collection of medieval art include the *Unicorn Tapestries*, priceless wall hangings depicting a hunt for a mythical white unicorn, which comes back to life when it is killed, and a medieval Book of Hours. Walking through the exhibition rooms is as much a religious, as historic, experience.

In 1658, Peter Stuyvesant established a trading post near the modern-day 125th Street, naming it "Nieuw Haarlem", after the Dutch town of Haarlem. German and Irish immigrants first settled here, followed by Italians. It was not until the beginning of the 20th century, when the subway was built, that African-Americans from Lower Manhattan also moved in. More African-Americans from the southern states and the West Indies followed during World War I, and since then Harlem has become the most famous black district in the United States. A focal point for the development of an

After the crash in 1929, Harlem became a slum. It was not until the late 1980s that a new mood emerged, which was described as "Harlem Renaissance". Today the district is no longer a slum. Even Bill Clinton, whom the black writer Toni Morrison, winner of the Nobel Prize for Literature, once described as "America's first black President", now has an office there.

independent black culture, it has also become a byword for the integration issues of the country's various communities, despite being in the supposed "melting pot" of New York. The election of Barack Obama as U.S. President has been the most important expression of a new black consciousness.

The Abyssinian Baptist Church is one of the most famous churches in Harlem and has at times been the home of the largest Protestant community in the United States. Its history dates back to the year 1808 when black believers left the First Baptist Church in the City of New York because it comprised an area designated for "Blacks only". In 1923 Adam Clayton Powell, the first vicar, moved with the community into a new church in what was then West 138th Street. He lured thousands of African-Americans to Harlem, preaching a social understanding of the gospel – combining spirit-

uality with social activities. His son, Adam Clayton Powell, Jr, himself a vicar and a civil rights activist, was the first delegate elected in New York as a member of Congress. The name of the church is based on an antiquated word for Ethiopia – the country from where the first community originated.

Built to the designs of Charles W. Bolton & Sons and completed in 1923, the Abyssinian Baptist Church (large picture) was located between Malcolm X Boulevard and the Adam Clayton Powell, Jr Boulevard, at what is now 132 Odell Clark Place (formerly 138th Street). The Baptist services with their moving gospel choirs are still one of Harlem's most famous tourist attractions (above).

Alongside New Orleans and Chicago, New York is major center of the jazz scene. In the 1920s Charlie "Bird" Parker, the legendary saxophonist, was lured from Chicago to New York where he appeared at Birdland, one of the first jazz clubs to open on Broadway. The jazz label *Blue Note* was also founded in New York. Numerous different styles of jazz, from BeBob and Swing to Free Jazz continued to be popular in the Big Apple. During the Prohibition period, it was mainly African-Americans who played at the legendary Cotton Club in Harlem for a white audience. One of the first stars was Duke Ellington. Owney Madden, who owned the club and was a an infamous gangster, had hired him in Philadelphia. "Pack your bag right now or you're dead!", he allegedly said to the Duke. The career of the unforgettable Billie Holiday began in a "speakeasy" (a type of bar where, during the Prohi-

Take the 'A' Train, once the Duke Ellington Band's signature tune, was an invitation people were more than happy to take up, as line A of the New York subway goes from Brooklyn directly to Harlem, right into the jazz-filled heart of the black community, where the blue notes resound in your ears. There's also lots of jazz at the Lenox Lounge (large picture and top right; above: one of the many clubs on Sugar Hill).

bition alcohol was illegally sold) in Harlem. "Lady Day", as she was known, was one of the most influential jazz singers of all time but only found real fame after her appearances at the Apollo Theater. This is where Ella Fitzgerald first enjoyed the limelight, also after a talent contest.

The legendary Apollo Theater, originally called "Hurtig and Seamon's Burlesque Theatre", opened on 125th Street in Harlem in 1914. Black people were not admitted at the time and only some twenty years later and after numerous changes in ownership were Afro-Americans allowed in to watch the performances. The Apollo Theater became famous thanks to the "Amateur Nights", a talent contest which took place every Wednesday and was broadcast live by 23 radio stations. Among the stars who emerging from the contests was Ella Fitzgerald, who had wanted to appear in a dance

act. Other great names include Billie Holiday, Aretha Franklin, Marvin Gaye, as well as the Jackson Five with Michael Jackson. In the 1960s and 1970s the Theater went into decline; it was then bought by the State of New York, made into a listed and protected monument, and reopened in 1985.

John Lennon knew why he wanted to go straight to the Apollo Theater on his first visit to New York. Elvis Presley, too, might have gathered inspiration here for the swing of his hips – the artists appearing at the Apollo Theater set the scene. Michael Jackson (large picture: fans in mourning after his death) also celebrated his first breakthrough here. Above: Doug E Fresh, the "human beat box".

New York 165

Harlem was once synonymous with racial tension, slum housing, and an economy built around illegal drugs. Now, times have changed – the recent opening of a Disney store on 125th Street, Harlem's main artery, proves that its past reputation had gone forever. There is as much bustle on 125th Street as on 42nd Street in Midtown, with McDonalds and Starbucks and traders selling rap albums. On a warm day, 125th Street offers visitors a cacaphony of rap, hip hop and house music. The Studio Museum is a window into the past and offers a fresh perspective to the future. At the

junction of 125th Street and 7th Avenue the Hotel Theresa recalls earlier times. Opened in 1913, and now an office building, it was here that Malcolm X met Muhammad Ali – and where Fidel Castro (1960, following an assembly of the United Nations in New York) met Khrushchev.

Harlem's lifeline is 125th Street, which is also known as Martin Luther King, Jr Boulevard (large picture). A statue commemorates the black member of Congress and civil rights activist Adam Clayton Powell, Jr (above). If you wish to see the "real" Harlem you should also explore the graffiti-covered side streets (top), with their clubs, stores, bistros, and restaurants.

The Unisphere, a giant globe, was set up for the World Exhibition in 1964. It stands near the Arthur Ashe Stadium in Queens, the stadium named after the first African-American member of the U.S. Davis Cup team.

Manhattan is not all there is to New York City; the four other boroughs also offer many attractions. Brooklyn is the jewel in their crown, and has some of the most beautiful parks, museums and brownstone buildings in New York City. The Bronx is now beginning to shake off its reputation of recent decades and while most people only know Queens from passing through from the airport, its galleries and sportsstadiums are worth visiting. Staten Island, with its ferry, is sometimes known as "the forgotten borough", but it boasts a greenbelt of 45 km (28 miles) of relaxing walking trails in a natural forest.

When the architect, John Roebling, a German immigrant, first raised the concept of the Brooklyn Bridge, most people regarded it as a folly. But he was determined to see the project through. A former bridge and road builder for the Prussian government, he came up with the plan after a ferry he had taken across the East River became stuck in ice. The most stunning place to view the bridge is from the River Café restaurant, on Brooklyn's waterfront, which has sweeping views over the Manhattan skyline and the Statue of Liberty. The owner, Michael O'Keeffe, also had to fight to launch his

DUMBO – "Down Under the Manhattan Bridge Overpass" – is the nickname given to the trendy port area of Brooklyn with its attractive lofts and stunning views of Manhattan. Today you can listen to gentle piano sounds while dining on excellent seafood – the restaurant has been awarded a Michelin star in 2010. When the River Café first opened none of the buildings were here; but the views have always been great.

restaurant which opened in the abandoned Brooklyn docks in 1977. Banks had refused to lend him money and business advsiors warned of bankruptcy. They were wrong and the restaurant, famed for its romantic atmosphere, was the catalyst for the successful redevelopment of the waterfront area.

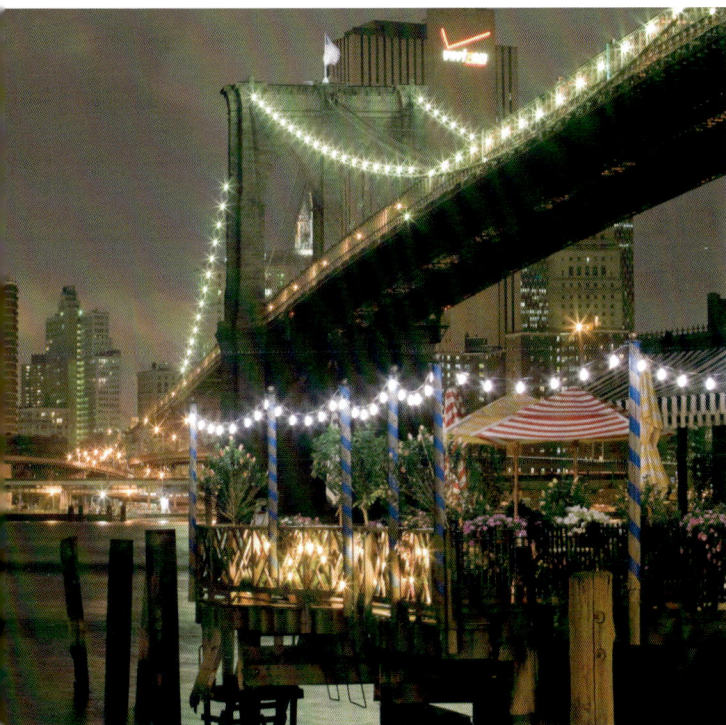

Manhattan's most attractive neighbor, Brooklyn is New York's most populous borough, with some 2.5 million residents. Until the five boroughs were incorporated in 1898, Brooklyn was the fourth-largest city in the country, and it still has a metropolitan mix: 93 different ethnic groups from 150 countries lived here at the end of the 1990s, with their identities emphasized by enclaves such as Little Odessa and Little Arabia. Brooklyn was originally named Breukelen after the town near Utrecht and began life as a Dutch settlement in 1636, just like Manhattan. Brooklyn Heights, an idyllic – and expen-

"I am a patriot", said Henry Miller, "of the 14th Ward Brooklyn, were I was raised. The rest of the United States doesn't exist for me, except as idea, or history, or literature." But you don't have to be a local patriot to find this district attractive; its typical brownstone houses (large picture) in Brooklyn Heights and the most attractive access route to Manhattan – across the Brooklyn Bridge. Top right: Brooklyn's waterfront.

sive – area at the mouth of the East River between Brooklyn Bridge and the Atlantic River, with beautiful brownstone buildings is listed as a national monument. Brooklyn Museum, one of the largest art galleries in the country, has a range of exhibits from Egyptian masterpieces to contemporary art.

Three bridges connect Brooklyn and Manhattan over the East River, their mnemonic being "BMW": starting from the north, Brooklyn, Manhattan, and Williamsburg. Entirely aware of its charms, Brooklyn Bridge, delivers the best views, including over the Brooklyn Promenade (also known as the Esplanade), which runs along the East River. One of Brooklyn's oldest public attractions, Prospect Park includes both the Brooklyn Museum and the Brooklyn Botanic Garden, was laid out in the 1860s. Its creators, Frederick Law Olmsted and Calvert Vaux, considered it a greater artistic success than

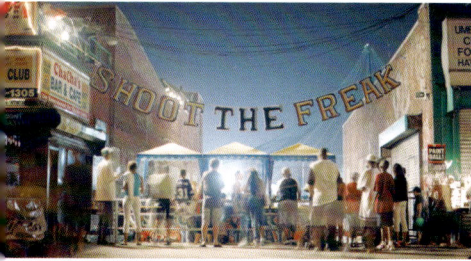

Central Park, which they had just designed and completed. The famous Coney Island peninsula in south Brooklyn, with its long beach and fairground, was a major day-trip destination in the late 19th and early 20th century for New Yorkers. Today, the fairground has a faded, nostalgic feel.

You might well find yourself humming "*Under the Boardwalk / Down by the sea / On a blanket with my baby / that's where I'll be*" by the Drifters, their 1964 Motown hymn of praise to the Coney Island boardwalks, the beach promenades that start right behind the subway lines. The nearby fairground (top) also gets a mention. In summer large crowds stroll along the promenade and it's not just dogs they take for a walk here (left).

OUTER BOROUGHS

Covering an area of 313 sq km (120 sq miles), Queens is New York's largest borough and there are supposedly more languages spoken here than anywhere else on earth. About half of the 2.2 million residents are of different ethnicities, so it seems appropriate that John F. Kennedy International and LaGuardia airports, two of the city's three international hubs, are located in the borough, which was founded in 1683 as a part of the English colony. Resonant names for sports fans include Shea Stadium (the home of the New York Mets baseball team until April 2009, when the new Citi Field

Stadium was opened) and the Arthur Ashe Stadium in Flushing Meadows Park, where the U.S. Tennis Open is held. Art fans will be drawn to MoMA's P.S.1 Contemporary Art Center, while the work of Japanese–American artist Isami Noguchi is on show at the Isami Noguchi Garden Museum.

Like Brooklyn, Queens is also located on Long Island, an Atlantic island extending parallel to the mainland over a length of 193 km (119 miles). Graffiti in the Queens looks different from that in the Bronx, more artistic and playful, less political; many a tagger may be thinking of themselves as a future Keith Haring – he first displayed his art in subway stations, long before he was recognized as museum-worthy.

The only borough of New York to have a definite article but an indefinite future – or so the joke went when the South Bronx ("SoBro") was a byword for urban decay with the highest crime rates in the United States. That was in the 1960s, but it had not always been the case. In 1639, when the Swedish seafarer Johan Bronck landed on the peninsula that was to be named after him, he felt he had discovered "a land of virgin forest and limitless opportunities". Despite its recent past, the Bronx is now on its way up again and has enjoyed an investment of almost $4.8 billion between

2002 and 2007 alone. The rich mix of diverse cultures who moved to the Bronx has resulted in a lively music scene – it is home to rap and hip hop. And the Bronx residents have every right to be proud. Their local heroes in pinstripes, the New York Yankees are giants in the world of baseball.

The restrained charm of sober functional structures (large picture: a bus depot) stands in marked contrast to the grand stadium of the New York Yankees, for example. Almost 25 percent of the residents (above at a snack stand) came from Puerto Rico, while an ever-growing number of immigrants nowadays arrive from Eastern Europe and Asia.

The New York Yankees are one of the most successful baseball clubs in the world. Founded in Baltimore (Maryland) in 1901 and initially known as Baltimore Orioles, they moved to New York two years later and changed their name to the New York Highlanders. The team became the New York Yankees, in 1913 when they began to play in the eastern division of the American League. With 26 World Series championships they are the most successful team in the United States. Their golden era began in 1920, when megastar Babe Ruth joined the Yankees and they replaced the New York Giants as the city's "number one team" at the new Yankee Stadium in the Bronx. When Babe left the Yankees in 1934, another superstar entered the scene, Joe DiMaggio. Until 1951 the "Yankee clipper", won the championships almost single-handedly; after his baseball

career ended he married Mary-lin Monroe. In the 1960s the team went into decline and they missed the playoffs several times. There were no new superstars. But in 1998 they celebrated a glorious come-back, and since 2009, have been playing in a new ground, the New Yankee Stadium.

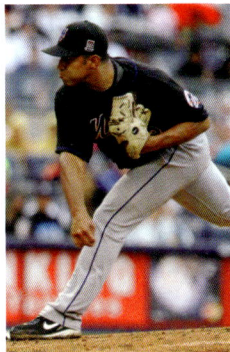

Since 2009 the New York Yan-kees (top: catcher Jorge Posada; above: pitcher Fernando Nieve) have played in a brand-new stadium that cost $1.5 billion to build (large picture). The team is also known as "heroes in pin-stripes" because of the stripes on their uniforms. When meet-ing the other team, however, the conduct is not necessarily gentlemen-like. You might even read on a poster: "Welcome to Da Bronx. Get ready to die!"

Founded in 1899, the Bronx Zoo was originally home to 843 animals; it now has more than 4000 animals and over 600 different species. The zoo was laid out in the 1880s and is part of the the gigantic Bronx Park. A botanical garden to the north was opened in 1891, based on the London Botanical gardens. The Peggy Rockefeller Rose Garden includes some 250 varieties of plants and in 1901 the Enid A. Haupt Conservatory opened, a Victorian greenhouse containing a tropical rainforest. The landmark Snuff Mill of 1840 recalls the garden's history. It once belonged to a snuff tobacco company. who used the

The largest urban zoo in the United States, the Bronx Wildlife Conservation Society, covers an area of some 107 ha (250 acres) and welcomes more than two million visitors each year (large picture: the gorilla enclosure). One of the rarest animals here is the snow leopard from Pakistan (above); it had lost its mother during a mudslide and was given a new home at the Bronx. Top right: orchids in flower at the Botanical Garden.

rose petals to perfume their tobacco. Now, more than 2,700 different rose varieties bloom today. The park includes an herbarium with over seven million species collected over three centuries. There is also an educational and activity centre where children can learn about plants and gardening.

New York is a pulsating city with many different faces. Towerng over the cityscape and an illuminated backdrop is the Empire State Building.

Is New York for culture lovers? Of course – there are museums and theaters galore. Is it a fantastic city for shopping? The variety of shops, from luxury boutiques to discount outlets, is enormous. A dream destination for gourmets? World-renowned chefs will take you on a culinary voyage of exploration. A haven for night owls? The "city that never sleeps" has clubs, bars, and discos for every taste. And if you need to rest, there's everything from the finest luxury hotel to the simplest hostel The following pages will give you expert tips on some of the best-known and must-see places in this unforgettable city.

The hexagonal shape of the Museum of Jewish Heritage reflects the Star of David.

MUSEUMS, MUSIC, DRAMA

George Gustav Heye Center (Museum of the American Indian) Dedicated to American Indian culture from North, South and Central America, the museum is housed in the old Custom House.
1 Bowling Green,
Tel 212-514-37 00,
www.nmai.si.edu,
10.00–17.00, daily,
Thurs 10.00–20.00.

The Grey Art Gallery New York University's gallery in the old NYU Silver Center concentrates on late 19th- and 20th-century art, including works by Picasso, Miró, Matisse, and American artists.
100 Washington Square East,
Tel 212-998-67 80,
www.nyu.edu/greyart/info,
Tues, Thurs, Fri 11.00–18.00,
Wed 11.00–20.00,
Sat 11.00–17.00.

Merchant's House Museum A townhouse of 1831 preserved in its original condition, affording a doorway into another world: the life of a well-to-do 19th-century New York merchant's family.
29 East Fourth Street,
Tel 212-777-10 89,
www.merchantshouse.com,
Thurs–Mon 12.00–17.00.

Museum of American Finance A glimpse into the world of American financial history and the stock exchange. It celebrates the spirit of entrepreneurship and the free market tradition.
48 Wall Street,
Tel 212-908-41 10,
www.moaf.org,
Tues–Sat 10.00–16.00.

Museum of Jewish Heritage Opened in 1997 in a six-sided, tiered building, the museum's photos, videos, documents, computer games, and exhibits are mostly concerned with the history of the Holocaust. However, they also deal with Jewish culture and lifestyle more generally, from the 19th century to the modern day.
36 Battery Place,
Tel 1-646-437-42 00,
www.mjhnyc.org,
Sun–Tues, Thurs 10.00–17.45,
Wed 10.00–20.00, Fri 10.00–15.00/17.00, closed Thanksgiving and Jewish holidays.

New Museum of Contemporary Art Founded in 1977, the museum features the latest trends in art. A great place for those interested in contemporary movements and in spotting new artists.
535 Broadway,
Tel 212-219-12 22,
www.newmuseum.org,
Wed, Sat, Sun 12.00–18.00,
Thurs, Fri 12.00–21.00,
closed Thanksgiving.

The New York City Fire Museum can tell a few exciting things about its heroic firefighters, and what they got up to since the 18th century.

New York City Fire Museum Housed in a fire station built in 1904, the museum has a wide range of exhibits, including fire apparatus, tenders, hoses, protective clothing, and parade uniforms, plus lots of interesting information about the New York Fire Department since the 18th century.
278 Spring Street,
Tel 212-691-13 03,
www.nycfiremuseum.org,
Tues–Sat 10.00–17.00,
Sun 10.00–16.00.

New York City Police Museum Three hundred years of the history of the police departments are brought to life here.
100 Old Slip,
Tel 212-480-31 00,
www.nycpolicemuseum.org,
Mon–Sat 10.00–17.00.

Skyscraper Museum The history and development of skyscraper construction tech-

niques, from their early beginnings up to the modern day, are illustrated in this museum.
39 Battery Place,
Tel 212-968-19 61,
www.skyscraper.org,
Wed–Sun 12.00–18.00.

South Street Seaport Museum Old businesses and warehouses in the original heart of New York's docks on the east shore of Manhattan have been partly converted into museums, with vintage sailboats, galleries, and pretty restaurants and cafés.
East River, 12 Fulton Street,
Tel 212-748-87 25,
www.southstreetseaport museum.org,
Apr–Dec Tues–Sun 10.00– 18.00, Jan–Mar Fri–Sun 10.00–17.00, sailings 12.00– 16.00 depending on weather.

Tenement Museum A working family's home from 1863, giving an idea of the far-from-

ideal but typical living conditions endured by the many immigrants of the period in New York.
97 Orchard Street,
Tel 212-431-02 33,
www.tenement.org,
10.15-17.00, daily, by guided tour only.

Trinity Museum A small museum in the left nave of Trinity Church, dealing with the history of the church community since the 17th century and the construction of the current neo-Gothic church.
Trinity Place,
Tel 212-602-08 00,
www.trinitywallstreet.org,
Mon–Fri 9.00–17.30,
Sat, Sun 9.00–15.45,
closed during services.

Ukrainian Museum Works by Ukrainian artists such as Alexander Archipenko and Alexis Gritchenko, plus Ukrainian folk

The peformances at the River to River Festivals in the parks and gardens between Battery Park and City Hall have become real tourist magnets.

art, including lace-making, Easter eggs, ceramics, and marriage customs.
222 E Sixth Street,
Tel 212-228-01 10,
www.ukrainianmuseum.org,
Wed–Sun 11.00–17.00.

FESTIVALS AND EVENTS

Halloween Parade The country's biggest Halloween celebrations take place on the streets of Greenwich Village, and especially in the streets around Sixth Avenue. The noisy after-party is held on Washington Square every year.
www.halloween-nyc.com,
31 Oct, from 19.00.

Howl! Festival A week-long festival presenting visual arts, drama, dance, film, and literary readings at various venues in the East Village.
Tel 212-673-54 33,
www.howlfestival.com, Aug.

Independence Day Fireworks The highlight of the US Independence Day celebrations is the great firework display on the East River, which is occasionally accompanied by a long procession of boats.
Tel 212-484-12 00,
http://nycgo.com,
21.00 on 4 Jul.

River to River Festival New York's biggest open-air festival comprises more than 500 events spread throughout the whole summer. The varied schedule includes live concerts ranging from classical to pop and jazz, dance and theatre performances, film showings, and much more.
www.rivertorivernyc.org,
Jun–Aug.

Washington Square Music Festival Free classical, jazz, and swing concerts held in the open air and performed by renowned musicians from Carnegie Hall, the Lincoln Center, the Metropolitan and New York City Operas, and the Brooklyn Academy of Music, as well as many other budding musicians. It is worth arriving early to get a good seat for the free concerts.
Tel 212-252-36 21,
www.washingtonsquare
musicfestival.org,
mid-Jun to mid-Jul.

SPORT, GAMES, FUN

Ringling Bros and Barnum & Bailey Circus The audience holds its breath at this exciting show, when daring acrobats show their skills on the trapeze and the high wire. The animals on show include "awesome elephants, beautiful big cats, gorgeous horses, and elegant exotics". The Ringling Brothers take animal welfare seriously and have established an

The Ringling Bros. and Barnum Bailey Circus with its exciting and varied show is one of the jewels in the circus tent.

elephant conservation center in central Florida in 1995. America's best clowns meanwhile always raise a laugh with their hilarious antics. The Ringling Brothers put on one of the finest circuses in America.
Madison Square Garden,
www.ringling.com,
Mid-Mar to the beginning of April.

Sydney's Playground Probably the largest playground in New York, with mini-skyscrapers, on which children can climb to their hearts' content, and toy vehicles to race round a replica highway. Sidney's Café nearby has all kinds of sweet and savory refreshments when the kiddies are tired out from too much fun – and of course for the parents too.
66 White Street,
Tel 212-431-91 25,
Mon, Wed, Fri 8.30–18.00,
Tues, Thurs, Sat 10.00–18.00.

HEALTH AND BEAUTY

Bunya City Spa This spa in SoHo offers Far Eastern-style relaxation, such as a papaya body polish, Japanese shiatsu, or a four-handed massage with Asiatic medicinal herbs.
474 West Broadway/Prince Street, Tel 212-388-12 88,
www.bunyacityspa.com,
Mon-Sat 10.00–21.00,
Sun 10.00–19.00.

Great Jones Spa This temple to relaxation promises that an afternoon spent in their Wet Lounge is better relaxation from daily stress than a week's holiday in the sunshine. In any case if you want to chill out this is the place to go.
29 Great Jones Street/Lafayette Street,
Tel 212-505-31 85,
www.gjspa.com,
Mon 16.00–22.00,
Tues–Sun 9.00–22.00.

Jivamukti For many this is the best place for yoga in Manhattan. Jivamukti yoga is taught to music, including pop and house, not just Indian or Far Eastern sounds.
841 Broadway/Union Square,
Tel 212-353-02 14,
www.jivamuktiyoga.com,
Mon–Thurs 8.00–20.00,
Fri 8.00–18.45, Sat–Sun 9.15–17.00.

Real Pilates Pilates guru Alycea Ungaro offers courses for beginners and advanced students alike.
177 Duane Street,
Tel 212-625-07 77,
www.realpilatesnyc.com,
Mon–Fri 8.00–19.00, Sat 9.00–13.00, Sun 9.15–14.00.

SHOPPING

Boucher The quirky design of the accessories made here by the storeowner, Laura Mady,

Economy Candy displays on its shelves a selection to please everyone with a sweet tooth.

has attracted plenty of customers to the Meatpacking District. Her necklaces and earrings are especially popular.
9 Ninth Avenue/Little West Street, Tel 212-206-37 75, Mar–Dec Mon–Sat 12.00–19.00, Sun 12.00-18.00, Jan–Feb closed Mon.

Century 21 The fashion discount store has four floors of designer clothes for him and her, from Armani and DKNY to Marc Jacobs, and other brands. Except for the early mornings, the store is always full as there are decent reductions.
22 Cortland Street/Church Street, Tel 212-227-90 92, www.c21stores.com, Mon–Wed and Fri 7.45–20.00, Thurs 7.45–20.30, Sat 10.00–20.00, Sun 11.00–19.00.

Daffy's Two floors of designer clothes and accessories for men, women, and children at exceptionally low prices (most reduced by 50 percent).
462 Broadway/Grand Street, Tel 212-334-74 44, www.daffys.com, Mon–Sat 10.00–20.00, Sun 12.00–19.00.

Dean & De Luca A SoHo delicatessen stocking Italian delights and provisions, and a wide range of kitchen utensils and gift ideas. The in-house espresso bar is very popular.
560 Broadway/Prince Street, Tel 212 226 68 00, www.deananddeluca.com, Mon–Fri 7.00–20.00, Sat, Sun 8.00–20.00.

Economy Candy Candy for young and old in a shop with jars full of gummy bears, licorice, and malt candy, plus chewing gum dispensers.
108 Rivington Street/Essex Street, Tel 212-254-15 31, www.economycandy.com, Sun–Fri 9.00–18.00, Sat 10.00–17.00.

Prada Along with the current collections you can also acquire earlier Prada pieces, but it's not just the fashion that will draw your attention. The building's interior is enthralling: the Dutch architect Rem Koolhaas has refashioned the old Guggenheim in SoHo into this flagship store.
575 Broadway, Tel 212-334-88 88, www.prada.com, Mon–Sat 11.00–19.00, Sun 12.00–18.00.

The Original Firestore Find souvenirs of New York Fire or Police Departments.
17 Greenwich Avenue/ Christopher Street, Tel 800-229-92 58, www.nyfirestore.com, Mon–Thurs 11.00–19.00, Fri–Sat 11.00–20.00, Sun 12.00–18.00.

With top chef Laurent Tourondel at **BLT Fish**, everything revolves around fish and seafood.

EATING AND DRINKING

Amaya A reliable Thai restaurant in the East Village. Don't let the somewhat kitsch atmosphere put you off: the crunchy pork ribs will make the trip worthwhile.
234 East Fourth Street
(near Avenue B),
Tel 646-313-19 87,
Mon–Thurs 12.00–23.00,
Fri–Sun 12.00–24.00.

Angelica Kitchen One of Manhattan's few vegetarian restaurants. Amongst the recommended dishes are the walnut and lentil pasties and the "Dragon Bowls".
300 East Twelfth Street
(corner Second Avenue),
Tel 212-228-29 09,
www.angelicakitchen.com,
11.30–22.30, daily.

Aroma Not much more than a classic diner with a few tables – but what a diner! Not every day grub, just the finest Italian dishes you can find.
36 East Fourth Street,
Tel 212-375-01 00,
www.aromanyc.com,
Sun–Thurs 17.00–23.00,
Fri, Sat 17.00–24.00.

Arturo's The best wood-oven pizza in town, according to real Italians. The salads are fresh and the wine is good too; there's even a very grand pizza topped with lobster.
106 W. Houston Street/
Ecke Thompson Street,
Tel 212 677-38 20,
Mon–Thurs 16.00–1.00,
Fri, Sat 16.00–2.00,
Sun 15.00–24.00.

Babbo One of the best Italians in Manhattan. Mario Batali, the head chef, indulges his guests with dishes such as goat's cheese tortellini and side dishes such as dried oranges and wild fennel pollen.
110 Waverly Place
(near Sixth Avenue),
Tel 212-777-03 03,
www.babbonyc.com,
Mon–Sat 17.30–23.30,
Sun 17.00–23.00.

Belcourt Matt Hamilton, the head chef, worked for a while on a Tuscan farm to get the right feel for traditional Italian food. He has invested his knowledge in the fine homemade food in this restaurant, complemented by its antique furniture.
84 East Fourth Street,
Tel 212-979-20 34,
Sun–Thurs 10.00–23.00,
Fri, Sat 10.00–24.00.

BLT Fish Proprietor and top chef Laurent Tourondel has described his fish restaurant as a "mixture of a Paris brasserie and a New England fish shack".
21 West 17th Street,
Tel 212-691-88 88,

Australian dishes and drinks are the menu hits at Bondi Road.

www.bltfish.com,
Mon–Thurs 11.45–14.30,
17.30–23.00, Fri 11.45–14.30,
17.30–23.30, Sat 17.30–23.30,
Sun 17.00–22.00.

Bondi Road The photos of Bondi Beach on the high walls here conjure up an Australian holiday feeling, and fish and chips, and other solid seafood dishes, are served up on rustic tables. The fish and the beer come from Australia and the bar is lively in the evenings.
153 Rivington Street
(near Suffolk Street),
Tel 212-253-53 11,
www.thesunburntcow.com,
Mon 16.00– 22.00, Tues, Wed 16.00– 24.00, Thurs 16.00–1.00, Fri 16.00–2.00, Sat 11.00–4.00, Sun 11.00–22.00.

Boqueria Inspired by the Boqueria market in Barcelona, this hip restaurant serves the apotheosis of Spanish cooking;

it's traditional yet innovative. The tapas and raciones taste even better than in Catalonia...
53 West 19th Street
(between Fifth and
Sixth Avenues),
Tel 212-255-41 60,
www.boquerianyc.com,
Mon–Thurs 12.00–24.00,
Fri, Sat 12.00–2.00.

Café Cordadito One of the few Cuban family restaurants with first-class, homemade food. The menu is dominated by meat with rice and beans in all their varieties.
210 East Third Street
(near Avenue B),
Tel 212-614-30 80,
Mon 17.00–23.00,
Tues–Fri 12.00–23.00,
Sat, Sun 11.00–23.00.

Café Katja Erwin Schrottner, an Austrian, has fulfilled a dream with this home-from-home bar. The menu lists Ber-

nerwurstel (sausages stuffed with Emmental), beetroot, and freshly baked pretzels.
79 Orchard Street
(corner Grand Street),
Tel 212-219-95 45,
www.cafe-katja.com,
16.00–1.00, daily.

Cherin Sushi A good-value sushi bar in the East Village – exceptional in expensive Manhattan. If you turn up for happy hour in the early evening, you'll get a discount.
306 East Sixth Street
(near Second Avenue),
Tel 212-388-13 48,
Mon–Thurs 17.00–24.00,
Fri, Sat 17.00–1.00.

Cones An Argentinean ice-cream bar with especially creamy ice cream in more than 20 varieties, plus many variations of sorbet.
72 Bleecker Street
(near Morton Street),

EN Japanese Brasserie serves freshly prepared tofu dishes with a variety of side dishes in elegant surroundings.

Tel 212-414-17 95,
Sun–Thurs 13.00–23.00,
Fri, Sat 13.00–1.00.

Dogmatic Dogs There are hot dogs on every corner in Manhattan, but these are good!!
26 East 17th Street
(near Broadway),
Tel 212-414-06 00,
Mon–Thurs 11.00–20.00,
Fri, Sat 11.00–21.00,
Sun 12.00-19.00.

Eat-pisode A jewel amongst the many Thai restaurants in New York. Wara Spulchai, the owner, has dispensed with any fussiness and relies on family recipes such as green chicken curry. The curry comes in five grades of heat.
123 Ludlow Street, (near Rivington Street), Tel 212-677-76 24, www.eat-pisode.com,
Mon–Thurs 12.00–23.00,
Fri, Sat 13.00–24.00,
Sun 14.00–23.00.

El Rinconcito A small Latin American diner with a family atmosphere. Salsa music gets you in the mood to eat roast chicken and enchiladas or pig's trotter stew.
408 East Tenth Street
(near Avenue C),
Tel 212-254-13 81,
9.00–21.00, daily.

EN Japanese Brasserie The first branch of a Japanese restaurant chain. Instead of the usual sushi and noodles they swear by fresh tofu in many variations with shrimp or thinly sliced meat (yuba).
435 Hudson Street
(corner Leroy Street),
Tel 212-647-91 96,
www.enjb.com,
Sun–Thurs 17.30–23.00,
Fri, Sat 17.30–24.00.

Eva's Tasty healthy food with a Mediterranean touch. The omelet shows how seriously the owners take healthy eating – it is only made with egg whites and is baked in the oven. Lovers of substantial fare swear by the turkey burgers. The freshly squeezed fruit juices are especially tasty. It's also available "to go".
11 West Eighth Street
(near Fifth Avenue),
Tel 212-677-34 96, www.evas-supplements.com,
Mon–Sat 11.00–23.00,
Sun 11.00–22.00.

Festival Mexicano Restaurant Forget the Tex-Mex food you get in most American "south of the border" restaurants – they have authentic Mexican cooking here, the best example of which is the hot chicken broth with chicken pieces and avocado. The meat and chicken tacos are also very good, and they have tasty milkshakes to soothe your palate.

The pizzas at Joe's Pizza are popular with everyone.

120 Rivington Street (near Essex Street), Tel 212-995-01 54, Sun–Thurs 11.00–23.00, Fri, Sat 11.00–24.00.

Frank One of the best Italians in the East Village. Famous for his hot sauces, Frank Prisinzano serves up some first-class homemade surprises.
88 Second Avenue (near Fifth Street), Tel 212-420-02 02, www.frankrestaurant.com, Mon–Thurs 10.00–1.00, Fri, Sat 10.00–2.00, Sun 10.00–24.00.

Georgia's Eastside BBQ Alan Natkiel learnt the secret art of the barbecue in Georgia. The ribs are marinated in beer before being grilled. There is also coleslaw, sweet vegetables, and cornbread.
192 Orchard Street (near Stanton Street),

Tel 212-253-62 80, www.georgias eastsidebbq.com, Mon 17.00–22.00, Tues–Sun 12.00–23.00.

Hong Kong Station A Chinese noodle restaurant of the first order. The egg or rice noodles are cooked in tasty chicken stock before the addition of mushrooms, broccoli or other treats, including cow's stomach and pig's blood, which takes some getting used to.
128 Hester Street (near Bowery), Tel 212-966-93 82, 7.30–20.30, daily.

Joe's Pizza An institution in Greenwich Village for years. Joe Pasquale, the owner, swears by original Italian thin-crust pizza with a balanced mixture of cheese and other toppings. Everything here is traditional, authentic, and satisfying.

7 Carmine Street (near Sixth Avenue), Tel 212-366-18 82, www.famousjoespizza.com, 9.00–5.00, daily.

La Paella A Latin atmosphere with cheerful music in a New York bodega, serving Spanish dishes such as the famed paella; five different versions are available.
214 East Ninth Street (near Third Avenue), Tel 212-598-43 21, Sun–Thurs 12.00–22.30, Fri, Sat 12.00–23.30.

Lavagna A romantic Italian in an unremarkable side street. The house specials include Margherita pizza from a wood oven, and fish dishes, too.
545 East Fifth Street, Tel 212-979-10 05, www.lavagnanyc.com, Mon–Thurs 18.00–23.00, Fri, Sat 18.00–24.00, Sun 17.00–23.00.

A shopping trip through Chinatown will make you hungry – how about Peking duck?

Moustache Middle Eastern cooking in a relaxed atmosphere. The salads are generous and fresh, and the pizzas and falafel will satisfy even the hungriest diners.
265 East Tenth Street
(near First Avenue),
Tel 212-228-20 22,
12.00–24.00, daily.

Pastis Typical Meatpacking District: this 1930s Paris brasserie has surprisingly authentic décor. Oysters, fish soup, artichokes, and first-class cocktails are amongst the regular customers' favorites.
9 Ninth Avenue,
Tel 212-929-48 44,
www.pastisny.com,
Mon–Wed 8.00–1.00,
Thurs 8.00–2.00, Sat 10.00–
3.00, Sun 10.00–1.00.

Peking Duck House Even the Chinese rate the Peking Duck, which tastes better than anywhere else in Chinatown. It is served here with pancakes, spring onions, gherkins, and Hoisin sauce. The chicken with pine kernels and Shanghai shrimp taste excellent, too.
28 Mott Street,
Tel 212-227-18 10,
www.pekingduckhousenyc.
com, Sun–Thurs 11.30–22.30,
Fri, Sat 11.45–23.00.

Prune One of the best places to go for an original lunch or weekend brunch. The sensational burgers and spaghetti carbonara are recommended and make a filling lunch or dinner in this quirky neighborhood restaurant.
54 East First Street,
Tel 212-677-62 21,
www.prunerestaurant.com,
Mon–Thurs 11.30–15.00,
18.00–23.00,
Fri 11.30–15.00, 18.00–24.00,
Sat 10.00–15.30, 18.00–24.00,
Sun 10.00–15.30, 17.00–22.00

Pylos Homemade Greek food, which compares favorably with the pseudo-Greek fare in other places. Lamb and chicken are cooked in a clay pot and there's a surprisingly wide range of Greek wines.
128 East Seventh Street
(near Avenue A),
Tel 212-473-02 20,
www.pylosrestaurant.com,
Mon, Tues 17.00–24.00,
Wed, Thurs, Sun 11.30–16.00,
17.00–24.00, Fri, Sat 11.30–
16.00, 17.00–1.00.

Red Egg The owner is the son of a Chinese father and a Peruvian mother and combines the best of each country's cuisine in an interesting fusion. ry the "curry bread bowl" with shrimp, chicken, pork, and vegetables.
202 Centre Street (corner
Howard Street),
Tel 212-966-11 23,
www.redeggnyc.com,
10.00–23.00, daily.

Govind Armstrong celebrates his creative cuisine in the bright and elegant Table 8.

Sapporo East A small Japanese bar without the elegance of the new East Village, and yet the slick feel is deceptive: the noodle dishes are excellent and the sushi here is pretty good too. Excellent value for money.
245 East Tenth Street (corner First Avenue),
Tel 212-260-13 30,
17.00–0.45, daily.

26 Seats The name comes from the 26 different chairs, but it is popular principally for its French-influenced food.
168 Avenue B,
Tel 212-677-47 87,
Tues–Thurs, Sun 17.30–23.00,
Fri, Sat 17.30–23.30.

Su Ra A hot tip for lovers of Korean food. Most visitors rave about the red snapper with mushrooms; the bibimbop (rice with vegetables and raw egg) and the noodle dishes are also excellent. For a reasonable price you can even have a "King's Meal" with a combination of various house specials.
105 East Ninth Street (near Fourth Avenue),
Tel 212-982-63 90,
www.suranyc.com,
Mon–Thurs 12.00–23.00,
Fri, Sat 12.00–24.00.

STK A trendy steak house in the Meatpacking District, decorated in black and silver and aiming for a female clientele. The steaks taste great.
26 Little West Twelfth Street (near Ninth Avenue),
Tel 646-624-24 44,
www.stkhouse.com,
17.30–2.00, daily.

11th Street Bar A traditional Irish pub with original Guinness and the alcoholic drinks that combine well with it.
510 East Eleventh Street (near Avenue A),
Tel 212-982-39 29,
Mon–Fri 16.00–4.00,
Sat, Sun 13.00–4.00.

Table 8 Govind Armstrong, an experimental cook from California, serves up surprising combinations of ingredients such as duck with candied kumquats, red snapper in lobster sauce, and filet mignon with leeks.
25 Cooper Square (near Sixth Street), Tel 212-475-34 00,
www.thecoopersquare hotel.com,
7.00–11.00, 12.00–15.30, 18.00–23.00, daily.

Texas Star Café Restaurant is a family owned business serving homemade specialties.
1606 N. 12th St., KS 66502,
Tel 785-539-93 93,
www.hibachihut.com,
Mon–Thurs 11.00–2100,
Fri, Sat 11.00–22.00, Sun 11.00–20.30, Tue closed.

The Cosmopolitan Hotel in New York's Tribeca district is in a great spot and affordable.

Tree A rustic bistro, with hearty down-to-earth, food. The intimate garden is a well-kept city secret.
190 FirstAvenue (near TwelfthStreet), Tel 212-358-71 71,
www.treenyc.com,
Mon–Thurs 17.00–24.00,
Fri, Sat 17.00–1.00, Sun 11.00–16.00, 17.00–24.00.

Tribeca Grill Top American cooking with an Asiatic and Italian touch, and the historic Tiffany bar is a good place to hang out in as well. Robert de Niro is the co-owner, and there are portraits of his father adorning the walls.
375 Greenwich Street/ (corner Franklin Street),
Tel 212-941-39 00,
www.myriadrestaurant group.com, Mon–Thurs 11.30–17.00, 17.30–23.00,
Fri to 23.30, Sun 11.30–15.00, 17.30–22.00.

wd-50 Wylie Dufresne, a celebrity chef with a love of experimentation, serves up exciting combinations. Pork belly and fish are among the top choices.
50 Clinton Street (near Rivington Street),
Tel 212-477-29 00,
www.wd-50.com,
Mon–Sat 18.00–23.00,
Sun 18.00–22.00.

Zoé A trendy SoHo hang-out. Modern American cuisine in Californian surroundings.
90 Prince Street, zwischen Broadway und Mercer Street,
Tel 212-966-67 22,
www.zoerestaurant.com,
Mon 12.00–15.00, Tues–Thurs 12.00–22.00, Fri 12.00–23.00,
Sat 11.30–15.30, 17.30–22.00.

ACCOMMODATION

Cosmopolitan Hotel A cozy hotel located in TriBeCa which is good value (for New York) at under $200, although you have to make certain allowances for the room size and low-scale furnishings.
95 West Broadway (near Chambers Street)
Tel 212-566-19 00,
www.cosmohotel.com

Duane Street Hotel A simple boutique hotel with sparsely decorated rooms that are mostly intended for business travelers. Guests can also take advantage of free admission to the nearby Tribeca Health & Fitness Club.
130 Duane Street (corner Church Street),
Tel 212-964-46 00,
www.duanestreethotel.com

Hampton Inn Manhattan-SoHo Hampton is one of the clean and reliable hotel chains in the United States. Usually reasonably priced, but the location in Manhattan means

Soft tones and dark wood characterize the interior at the 60 Thompson.

you will have to dig a little deeper here. The terrace on the 19th floor offers visitors a great view of New York.
54 Watts Street (near Sixth Avenue), Tel 212-226-62 88, www.hamptonsohonyc.com

Holiday Inn Express Downtown You know what you are getting; one of the best-value and most reliable hotel chains in the country; large rooms, comfortable beds, basic design.
126 Water Street, Tel 212 747 92 22, www.hiexpress.com

Hotel on Rivington A futuristic-looking hotel in a glass and aluminum high-rise. The rooms were styled in black and white by the designer India Mahdavi and have strikingly large windows.
107 Rivington Street, Tel 212-475-26 00, www.hotelonrivington.com

Lafayette House An unassuming guesthouse in an historic 1840s brownstone house. The variously decorated rooms and friendly welcome make you feel right at home in New York. The rooms are luxurious, the beds comfortable, and there is a welcoming open fire.
38 East Fourth Street (near Bowery), Tel 212-505-8100, www.lafayettenyc.com

The Mercer Film stars, models, and other celebrities discovered this hotel in SoHo long ago. The rooms are elegantly decorated with striking flowing lines. The showers are enormous, the bathtubs are big enough for two, and the toiletries in the bathrooms are from a leading Swedish cosmetics firm.
147 Mercer Street (near Prince Street), Tel 212-966-60 60, http://mercerhotel.com

Second Home on Second Avenue Five astonishingly large rooms in a simple guesthouse in the East Village. The Peruvian owner has drawn on the folklore of his South American homeland for the décor. The beds are comfortable, and the service extremely friendly.
221 Second Avenue (near 14th Street), Tel 212-677-31 61

SoHotel You have to make a lot of allowances for the room rates at this hotel: the rooms are small and sparsely furnished, the corridors narrow, and the service limited, but the prices are great.
341 Broome Street (near Bowery), Tel 212-226-14 82, www.thesohotel.com

60 Thompson A modern boutique hotel located in SoHo that isn't just for rich brokers

Jazz legends like Lionel Hampton, Sarah Vaughan, and Oscar Peterson have all appreciated the intimate ambience of the Blue Note.

and beautiful models. The top floor is taken up with "a60," a Moroccan-themed club with great views over the city.

60 Thompson Street
(near Broome Street),
Tel 212-219-20 00,
www.60thompson.com

Washington Square Hotel
Writers, singers, and artists, including Bob Dyland and Joan Bez, lived in this hotel in the West Village in the 1960s; the hotel has since been renovated.

103 Waverly Place
(near MacDougal Street),
Tel 212-777-95 15,
www.washington
squarehotel.com

NIGHTLIFE

2A This popular bar in the East Village has been here since the 1980s. The drug dealers have moved out of the area and now there are restaurants and

bistros with a middle-class clientele. You get two drinks for the price of one between 16.00 and 20.00.

25 Avenue A (corner Second Street), Tel 212-505-24 66, 16.00–4.00, daily.

Blue Note Since opening in 1981, Blue Note has become one of the most successful jazz clubs in the world, with intimate surroundings.

131 West Third Street,
www.bluenote.net,
Tel 212-475-85 92,
from 20.00, daily.

5C Cafe and Cultural Center A health food restaurant by day; a jazz club by night, this has remained an insider tip despite its successful concerts.

68 Avenue C (corner Fifth Street), Tel 212-477-59 93, www.5ccc.com, Tues–Thurs 17.00–21.00, Fri, Sat 17.00–1.00.

Entwine A spacious and cozy wine bar in the West Village. Excellent selection of wines from all over the world, at a price to suit everyone.

765 Washington Street (near Twelfth Street),
Tel 212-727-87 65,
www.entwinenyc.com,
Sun–Thurs 15.00–24.00,
Fri, Sat 15.00–2.00.

White Horse Tavern The Welsh poet and writer Dylan Thomas's former hangout, and still a shrine for fans and followers of the famous poet. His death was supposedly related to the 18 whiskies he had enjoyed in this bar. The range of whiskeys on sale here is appropriate to such an historic place where the literary muse still lives.

567 Hudson Street
(corner Eleventh Street),
Tel 212-243-92 60,
11.00–3.00, daily.

Carnegie Hall boasts a great variety of events from classical music to pop concerts as well as a small exhibtion, the Rose Museum, and a picture gallery.

MUSEUMS, MUSIC, DRAMA

American Folk Art Museum Housed in a spectacular new building by Tod Williams and Billie Tsien, the museum is devoted to American life from the colonial period to the present day. Exhibits include drawings, paintings, sculpture, photographs, and everyday objects from all walks of life.
45 West 53rd Street,
Tel 212-265-10 40,
www.folkartmuseum.org,
Tues–Sun 10.30 17.30,
Fri 10.30–19.30.

American Museum of the Moving Image Founded in 1988 in a building belonging to Astoria Studios, the museum exhibits film and video pieces by contemporary artists as well as giving an overview of the origins and history of cinema. Exhibits include equipment, movie props, and nostalgia.

35th Avenue, 37th Street,
Tel 718-784-45 20,
www.movingimage.us,
Tues–Fri 10.00–15.00.

Carnegie Hall A neo-Renaissance building with three concert halls. The Isaac Stern Auditorium, containing almost 2,800 seats and with excellent acoustics is famous. It was built in 1891 thanks to a generous donation from Andrew Carnegie, the steel magnate, and was once the home of the New York Philharmonic, which has since moved on to the Lincoln Center.
881 Seventh Avenue,
Tel 212-632-05 40,
www.carnegiehall.org

International Center of Photography Museum The ICP Museum opened in 1974, and the temporary exhibitions that it holds are drawn from its more than 10,000 photographs.

1133 Avenue of the Americas, Tel 212-857-00 00,
www.icp.org,
Tues–Thurs, Sat, Sun 10.00–18.00, Fri 10.00–20.00.

Intrepid Sea Air Space Museum The aircraft carrier USS Intrepid, which saw service in World War II, has been used as a museum ship since 1982. You can see military aircraft, helicopters, and U.S. space program items. There is also a nuclear submarine, the Growler, and a French/British Concorde.
Pier 86, Twelfth Avenue/ 46th Street,
Tel 877-957-74 47 (SHIP),
www.intrepidmuseum.org,
Apr to Sep Mon–Fri 10.00–17.00, Sat, Sun, public hols, 10.00–18.00, Oct–Mar Tues–Sun 10.00–17.00.

Madison Square Garden This famous multi-purpose complex contains a large sports arena

Great sports events as well as concerts of megastars in the rock world are held at the Madison Square Garden.

where rock concerts and sporting events such as basketball, ice hockey, and boxing matches all take place.
4 Pennsylvania Plaza,
Tel 212-465-67 41,
www.thegarden.com

The Museum at FIT The museum is part of the State University of New York's Fashion Institute of Technology and takes visitors on a fascinating stroll through the history of fashion from the 18th century to the present day.
Tel 212-217-45 58,
www.fitnyc.edu/museum,
Tues–Fri 12.00–20.00,
Sat 10.00–17.00.

Pierpont Morgan Library This library building was opened to the public in 1924 as a gift from J P Morgan, one of America's richest men. Themed temporary exhibitions and the permanent exhibition drawn from its own holdings give an overview of the world of medieval manuscripts and incunabula. There are manuscripts by Charles Dickens, Mozart, Lord Byron, and Robert Burns, among many others.
225 Madison Avenue/36th Street, Tel 212-685-00 08,
www.themorgan.org,
Fri 10.30–21.00, Sat 10.00–18.00, Sun 11.00–18.00.

The Museum of Television and Radio Here you can listen to the news on the radio and watch TV shows right from the very early days up to the present day. Make your choice among some 50,000 rolls of films and radio recordings and wallow in nostalgia of days gone by.
25 West 52nd Street
Tel 212-621-66 00,
www.paleycenter.org,
Wed and Fri–Sun 12.00–18.00, Thurs 12.00–20.00.

Rubin Museum of Art Opened in 2004, the museum is devoted to the culture of the Himalayan region.
150 W 17th Street,
Tel 212-620-50 00,
www.rmanyc.org,
Mon, Thurs 11.00–17.00, Wed 11.00–19.00, Fri 11.00–22.00, Sat, Sun 11.00–18.00.

Theodore Roosevelt Birthplace An early 20th-century reconstruction of the original brownstone, the house is full of mementos of the U.S. president, who was born in New York in 1858.
28 East 20th Street,
Tel 212-260-16 16,
www.nps.gov,
Tues–Sat 9.00–17.00.

FESTIVALS AND EVENTS

9th Avenue International Food Festival Every year, up to a million visitors are drawn

New York's largest Christmas tree and countless lights create a festive mood at the Rockefeller Center.

to the culinary delights offered by the festival. There is also a flea market, bric-a-brac, market stalls, and live music.
Ninth Avenue on West
Fifth–37th Street,
Tel 212-484-12 00,
http://nycgo.com, mid-May.

Christmas Tree Lighting Ceremony In a festive ceremony at the Rockefeller Center the lights are lit on New York's largest Christmas tree.
Fifth Avenue between West
49th and 51st Street,
Tel 212-632-39 75,
www.rockefellercenter.com,
late Nov/early Dec.

Columbus Day Parade More than 500,000 spectators gather on Fifth Avenue to remember explorer Christopher Columbus.
Fifth Avenue from East 44th
to 79th Street,
www.columbuscitizensfd.org,
around 12 Oct.

Easter Parade Participants flock to St Patrick's Cathedral for this special Easter event, showing off their magnificent, and occasionally rather daring, Easter hats, bonnets, and other headgear
5th Avenue between East
50th and 51st Street,
www.saintpatricks
cathedral.org,
Easter Sunday, 10.00–16.00.

Fleet Week A week-long celebration of the Navy, Marine Corps, and Coast Guard which sees New York City invaded by hundreds of sailors looking for a party; the climax of Fleet Week is the remembrance service for fallen US service personnel, which is held on the aircraft carrier Intrepid on Memorial Day.
West 46th St/Twelfth Avenue,
Tel 212-245-00 72,
www.intrepidmuseum.com,
late May.

Gay and Lesbian Pride Parade The lesbian and gay pride parade moves down Fifth Avenue in a five-hour spectacle with dancers, drag queens, gay construction workers, leather-wearing men, lesbian policewomen, and many others.
From Columbus Circle via
Fifth Avenue to Christopher
Street, Tel 212-807-74 33,
www.nycpride.org,
last Sun in Jun.

New Year's Eve New Year's Eve celebrations begin at 19.00 in Times Square. The countdown until the Waterford crystal ball raised on a pole over One Times Square is dropped at midnight has become world-famous.
www.timessquarenyc.org

Puerto Rican Day Parade Thousands of dancing and flag-waving spectators line Fifth and Third Avenues to see

New York has a cable car too: the Roosevelt Island Tram gives passengers a fabulous view of the Manhattan skyline during the four-minute ride.

the Puerto Rican parade with its traditional dance troupes and musicians.
Fifth to Third Avenue from East 44th to 86th St, www.nationalpuertorican dayparade.org, 2nd Sun in Jun.

St Patrick's Day Parade

Spectators descend on Fifth Avenue in their thousands to cheer on the world-famous Irish procession of bagpipers.
Fifth Avenue from East 44th St, www.saintpatricksday parade.com, 17 Mar.

SPORT, GAMES, FUN

Annual Empire State Building Run Up The annual run up the stairs of the Empire State from the lobby to the 86th floor comprises 1,576 steps. Experienced runners can do it in about nine minutes.

350 Fifth Avenue/34th Street, Tel 212-736-31 00, www.esbnyc.com, Feb.

Chelsea Piers Sports and Entertainment Complex A trip to the city's largest leisure and sports complex might tempt you – there are facilities for ball games (baseball, soccer, golf) and martial arts plus boxing, along with swimming, yoga, climbing, and much more. There are also two rinks for skating and ice hockey, and also an outdoor roller-blading area.
Pier 59–62, 23rd Street/West Side Highway, Tel 212-336 66 66, www.chelseapiers.com

Roosevelt Island Tram The aerial tram, generally just known as "the tram", starts in Manhattan at the intersection of 2nd Avenue and 60th Street, crosses the East Channel of the

East River at a height of 40 m (130 ft) and terminates on Roosevelt Island after a journey of about 1 km (half a mile).
Roosevelt Island Operating Corporation, Tel 212-832-45 55, www.rioc.com,

HEALTH AND BEAUTY

Bliss49 You can switch off from daily stress here, either in the sauna, under a steam shower, or with a massage.
541 Lexington Avenue/East 49th Street, Tel 212-219-89 70, www.blissworld.com, 8.00–22.00, daily.

Elizabeth Arden's Red Door If you have a large enough wallet, pamper yourself and visit the Red Door Salon & Spa. The range of treatments on offer includes anything from ranges of facials to steam

The NBA Store is an absolute must-see for baseketball fans.

baths and massages, in addition to perfect manicures and pedicures.
691 Fifth Avenue/54th Street, Tel 212-546-02 00, www.reddoorspas.com

Okeanos "A day at the Banya is a day without ageing", so goes the motto at this Russian spa in Midtown East. Enjoy a traditional steam-infused Russian sauna – the authentic Platza ritual involves being hit repeatdedly with branches of birch tree.
211 East 51st Street/Third Avenue, Tel 212-223-67 73, www.okeanosclubspa.com, Tues–Fri 12.00–22.00, Sat 11.00–20.00, Sun to 17.00.

The Avon Salon & Spa Located in the Trump Tower, the salon of this large U.S. cosmetics company offers health and beauty treatments in a pleasant environment.

1345 5th Avenue/East 56th Street, Tel 212-755-28 66

SHOPPING

Christie's The auctions at Christie's are always considered a big social event.
20 Rockefeller Plaza/West 49th Street, Tel 212-636-20 00, www.christies.com, Mon–Fri 9.30–17.30.

Emporio Armani If you like Armani designer clothes, this is the place to be. Relax in the café on the sixth floor.
601 Madison Avenue/ East 56th Street, www.emporioarmani.com, Mon–Sat 10.00–19.00, Sun 12.00–18.00.

Lord & Taylor The most traditional retailer of ladies' and gentlemen's clothing in the United States is based near the

Empire State Building.
424 Fifth Avenue, Tel 212-391-33 44, www.lordandtaylor.com, Mon–Fri 10.00–20.30, Sat 10.00–19.00, Sun 11.00–19.00.

Manolo Blahnik It has to be high heels: platforms and quirky design made this Spanish designer's shoes a status symbol.
31 West 54th Street/Fifth Avenue, Tel 212-582-30 07, www.manoloblahnik.com, Mon–Fri 10.30–20.00, Sat 10.30–17.30, Sun 12.00–17.00.

NBA Store A world of excitment for basketball fans in the National Basketball Association's (NBA) only store in New York city.
666 Fifth Avenue/West 52nd Street, Tel 212–515 62 21, www.nba.com, Mon–Sat 10.00–19.00 (summer 10.00–20.00), Sun 11.00–18.00.

Tourneau Time Machine is the self-proclaimed largest clock store in the world, selling more than 8000 different timepieces.

The Original Levi's Store The right place to stock up on original Levi's. As well as jeans there are shirts, T-shirts, sweaters, jackets, and accessories.
750 Lexington Avenue/59th Street, Tel 212-826-59 57, www.levi.com, Mon–Sat 10.00–20.00, Sun 12.00–18.00.

Tourneau Time Machine The three floors of this veritable temple to time are stocked with over 90 brands.
12 East 57th Street/Fifth Avenue, Tel 212-758-7300, www.tourneau.com, Mon–Wed and Fri–Sat 10.00–18.00, Thurs 10.00–19.00, Sun 11.30–17.30.

Toys "R" Us The largest U.S. branch of this toy chain is chock full of children – especially in the run-up to Christmas.
1514 Broadway, Tel 800-869-77 87,
www.toysrus.com, Mon–Sat 10.00–22.00, Sun 11.00–20.00.

EATING AND DRINKING

Abboccato Head chef Jake Addeo has a predilection for extraordinary Italian food, conjuring exquisite Italian nouvelle cuisine from quite rustic ingredients.
136 West 55th Street (near Sixth Avenue), Tel 212-265-40 00, www.abboccato.com, Mon 7.30–10.30, 12.00–15.00, 17.00–22.00, Tues–Sat 7.30–10.30, 12.00–15.00, 17.00–23.00, Sun 7.30–10.30, 16.00–22.00.

Adour Alain Ducasse This gourmet paradise in the St Regis Hotel is decorated in rich mahogany and burgundy tones Alain Ducasse has won Michelin stars and can turn even the simplest of root vegetables into a culinary delicacy.
2 East 55th Street (corner Fifth Avenue), Tel 212-710-22 77, Sun–Thurs 17.30–22.30, Fri, Sat 17.30–23.00.

Alonso's Steakhouse This tiny steak and seafood restaurant is not just out of the ordinary because of the stuffed ox, elk, and bear heads. It has also become well known for its excellent and juicy Porterhouse steaks.
265 West 20th Avenue (near Eight Avenue), Tel 212-675-77 49, www.chelseadining.com, 17.00–23.00, daily.

Aquavit Enoy Hypermodern surroundings and aquavit in this smart Scandinavian restaurant. The specialties include herring (of course) served with vodka and "beef Rydberg"

DB Bistro Moderne has a different kind of burger on offer, and at easy-to-digest prices.

(steak with onions served with a raw egg).
*65 East 55th Street
(near Madison Avenue),
Tel 212-307-73 11,
www.aquavit.org,
Sun–Thurs 12.00–14.30,
17.30–22.30, Fri 12.00–14.30,
17.15–23.00, Sat 17.00–23.00.*

Ariana Afghan Kebab House
One of the smallest but best kebab restaurants in Midtown.
*787 Ninth Avenue
(near 52nd Street),
Tel 212-262-23 23,
12.00–22.45, daily.*

Artisanal A bistro with a very French atmosphere, making you feel as if you're in the middle of Paris. The focus here is on cheeses, and over 200 different varieties from around the world are on offer here.
*2 Park Avenue (corner 32nd Street), Tel 212-725-8585,
www.artisanalcheese.com,*

Mon–Fri 10.45–22.45, Sat 10.30–22.45, Sun 10.30–22.00.

Bao Noodles Co-owner Michael Huynh has brought the recipes of his youth to New York. The stir-fries, noodles, and salads taste just like they do in the Far East. He also serves an selection of very tasty dressings.
*391 Second Avenue
(near 23rd Street),
Tel 212-725-77 70,
www.baonoodles.com,
Sun–Wed 11.30 23.00, Thurs–Sat 11.00–24.00.*

Beacon All the dishes are cooked or grilled over an open fire: trout, duck, and even the oyster.s
*25 West 56th Street
(near Fifth Avenue),
Tel 212-332-05 00,
www.beaconnyc.com,
Mon–Thurs 12.00–14.30,
17.00–22.00, Fri 12.00–14.30,*

*17.00–22.30, Sat 17.00–22.30,
Sun 10.30–14.30, 16.00–20.00.*

Better Burger Fast food for vegetarians and the health-conscious in Manhattan.
*561 Third Avenue (near 37th Street), Tel 212-949-75 28,
www.betterburgernyc.com,
Mon–Sat 11.00–22.30,
Sun 11.00–22.00.*

BLT Steak BLT only have supporting roles. The main part is played by the excellent steak; amazingly tender filet mignon.
*106 East 57th Street
(near Park Avenue),
Tel 212-752-74 70,
www.bltsteak.com,
Mon–Thurs 11.45–14.30,
17.30–23.00, Fri 11.45–14.30,
17.30–23.30, Sat 17.30–23.30.*

Boi This Vietnamese restaurant has an excellent menu and has won praise from the Vietnamese community.

Estiatorio Milos spoils his guests with tasty and refined Greek cooking.

246 East 44th Street (near Second Avenue), Tel 212-681-65 41, www.boirestaurant.com, Mon–Wed 11.30–15.00, 17.30–22.00, Thurs, Fri 11.30– 15.00, 17.30–23.00, Sat 17.30– 23.00, Sun 17.00–21.00.

Burger Joint No longer an insider tip: the burgers in this upscale burger bar in the lobby of the Parker Meridien Hotel taste out of this world.
119 West 56th Street (near Sixth Avenue), Tel 212-708-74 14, www.parkermeridien.com, Sun–Thurs 11.00–23.30, Fri, Sat 11.00–24.00.

Carve Unique Sandwiches A sandwich shop in the Theater District for the upper crust.
760 Eigth Avenue (corner 47th Street), Tel 212-730-49 49, 7.00–17.00, daily.

Cookshop The open-plan kitchen of this very trendy restaurant in Chelsea always serves up healthy, but hearty fare such as grilled chicken and steamed fish.
156 Tenth Avenue (corner 20th Street), Tel 212-924-44 40, www.cookshopny.com, Mon–Fri 11.30–15.00, 17.30– 24.00, Sat 11.00– 15.00, 17.30–24.00, Sun 11.00–15.00, 17.30–22.00.

Darbar Grill The atmosphere is reminiscent of a traditional upscale steak house, but head chef Simon Gomes always cooks delicious light Indian cuisine with an international feel. twist.
157 East 55th Street (near Third Street), Tel 212-751-46 00, www.darbargrillny.com, Sun–Thurs 11.30–22.30, Fri, Sat 11.30–23.00.

DB Bistro Moderne Daniel Bouloud ("DB"), the head chef serves up an alternative to the usual "whoppers": his "DB" burger is stuffed with truffle and foie gras.
55 West 44th Street (near Fifth Avenue), Tel 212-391-24 00, www.danielnyc.com, Mon 7.00–10.00, 12.00–14.30, 17.00–22.00, Tues–Fri 7.00– 10.00, 12.00–14.30, 17.00– 23.00, Sat 8.00–11.00, 12.00– 14.30, 17.00–23.00, Sun 8.00–11.00, 17.00–22.00.

Django There's no spaghetti Western food here, but rather tapas and Italian snacks, with first class wine, crusty bread and a selection of dips.
480 Lexington Avenue (corner 46th Street), Tel 212-871-66 00, www.django-gorestaurant.com, Mon–Fri 11.30–14.00, 17.30– 22.30.

You can even enjoy German and Austrian food in New York, at the Klee Brasserie for example.

Estiatorio Milos Fine fare from Greece, washed down with excellent Greek wines, in pleasant surroundings.
*125 West 55th Street
(near Sixth Avenue),
Tel 212-245-74 00,
www.milos.ca,
Mon–Fri 12.00–14.45, 17.00–23.45, Sat 17.00–23.45,
Sun 17.00–22.45*

99c Fresh Pizza Exactly what it says on the sign: Abdul's pizza really costs only 99 cents.
*151 East 43rd Street
(near Third Avenue),
Tel 212-922-02 57,
Mon–Sat 9.00–2.30,
Sun 12.00–2.30.*

Go! Go! Curry The Japanese baseball star Hideki Matsui wore the number 55 on his jersey and has named his Asian restaurant accordingly: "Go! Go!" means "55" in Japanese. Curry is the order of the day.

*273 West 38th Street
(near Eighth Avenue),
Tel 212-730-55 55,
10.55–21.55, daily.*

Hallo Berlin Authentic German and Austrian cuisine, a rare thing in the United States, with Wiener schnitzel, sausage dishes, dumplings, and rollmops (pickled herring) on the menu – almost like being in Germany itself.
*626 Tenth Avenue (near 44th Street), Tel 212-977-19 44,
www.halloberlin
restaurant.com,
Sun–Thurs 12.00–23.00,
Fri, Sat 12.00–1.00.*

Klee Brasserie This bistro has an interesting selection of German and Austrian dishes, with beer from Cologne and Belgium. Recommended: roast lamb and the varied poultry dishes.
200 Ninth Avenue (near 22nd Street), Tel 212-633-80 33,

*www.kleebrasserie.com,
Tues–Fri 12.00–15.00, 17.30–24.00, Sat 11.00–15.30, 17.30–24.00, Sun 11.00–15.30,
17.00–22.00.*

Kurumazushi Sinfully expensive, but worth every cent. Toshihiru Uezu's unassuming portion of sushi heaven is famous for its top tuna sashimi and its incomparable uni (sea urchin).
*7 East 47th Street (on the 2nd floor of an office block),
Tel 212-317-28 02,
Mon–Sat 11.30–14.00, 17.30–22.00.*

La Grenouille This restaurant is in an elegant room filled with bright flowers where you immediately feel at home. Charles Masson, the owner, celebrates French cuisine – the fish dishes are wonderful.
*3 East 52nd Street (near Fifth Avenue),
Tel 212-752-14 95,*

Visit Le Périgord and enjoy the finest of French cuisine.

www.la-grenouille.com, Tues–Sat 12.00–15.00, 17.00–23.00.

La Petite Auberge A real insider tip among the better French restaurants. You'll get a good value, top-class three-course meal here.
116 Lexington Avenue (corner 28th Street), Tel 212-689-50 03, www.lapetiteaubergeny.com, Oct–May Mon–Fri 12.00–23.00, Sat 17.00–23.00, Sun 16.30–22.00, Jun–Sep Tues–Fri 12.00–23.00, Sat 17.00–23.00.

Lazzara's Pizza Café A slightly out-of-the-way restaurant but popular with pizza fans since 1985. The pizza here is as thin and crispy as they eat it in Sicily with a wide choice of toppings.
221 West 38th Street (near Seventh Avenue), Tel 212-944-77 92,

www.lazzaraspizza.com, Mon 11.30–16.30, Tues–Fri 11.30–21.00.

Le Périgord An elegant French restaurant with fine cooking. Among the recommended dishes here are classics like veal kidneys with mustard sauce or roast salmon with ratatouille.
405 East 52nd Street, Tel 212-755-62 44, www.leperigord.com, Mon–Fri 12.00–15.30, 17.30–22.00, Sat, Sun 17.30–22.00.

Le Zie Italian home cooking as it should be: hearty spaghetti with meatballs, delicious lasagne, linguini, and wonderful fish dishes are all featured on the menu.
172 Seventh Avenue (near 20th Street), Tel 212-206-86 86, www.lezie.com, Mon–Fri 12.00–23.30, Sat, Sun 12.00–23.00.

Los Dos Molinos Fans of spicy Mexican food have picked the right place. Pork ribs with rice and beans are recommended.
119 East 18th Street (near Park Avenue South) Tel 212-505-15 74, www.losdosmolinosnyc.com, Tues–Thurs 12.00–14.30, 17.00–22.30, Fri 12.00–14.30, 17.00–23.30, Sat 15.00– 23.30, Sun 12.00–17.00.

Mia Dona A tiny and rather cramped restaurant but with first-class Mediterranean cuisine. The grilled lamb and quail brochette and roasted rabbit are amongst the best choices on the menu.
206 East 58th Street (corner Third Avenue), Tel 212-750-81 70, www.miadona.com, Mon–Thurs 12.00–14.30, 17.00–22.00, Fri 12.00–14.30, 17.00–23.00, Sat 17.00– 23.00, Sun 11.00–14.30, 17.00–21.00.

The venerable Algonquin Hotel was the gathering point for New York's intelligentsia in the 1920s.

Norma's The breakfast and lunch menu at the Le Parker Meridian hotel has gained world-wide notoriety for its legendary $1,000 omelet (served with lobster and unlimited beluga caviar).
118 West 57th Street
(near Sixth Avenue),
Tel 212-708-74 60,
www.normasnyc.com,
7.00–15.00, daily.

Omai A very good Vietnamese in Chelsea where the head chef cooks for demanding fans of Asian cooking.
158 Ninth Avnue
(near 19th Street),
Tel 212-633-05 50,
www.omainyc.com,
12.00–14.30, 17.30–22.00,
daily.

Pom Pom Diner This diner has been a regular stop for hungry walkers and night owls since 1969. Traditional American fast food such as cheeseburgers and club sandwiches are amongst the most popular orders.
610 Eleventh Avenue
(near 45th Street),
Tel 212-397-83 95
Mon–Sat 24 hours.

Prespa Most customers prefer to sit at the long bar. A relaxed atmosphere and pleasant guitar music accompany great-tasting and inventive dishes.
184 Lexington Avenue
(near 31st Street),
Tel 212-810-43 35,
www.prespanyc.com,
12.00–23.00, daily.

Quality Meats One of the many first-class steak houses in Manhattan. The giant steaks are excellent.
57 West 58th Street
(near Sixth Avenue),
Tel 212-371-77 77,
www.qualitymeatsnyc.com,
Mon–Wed 11.30–15.00,
17.00–22.30, Thurs, Fri 11.30–
15.00, 17.00–23.00, Sat 17.00–
23.00, Sun 17.00–22.00.

Sparks One of the best steak houses in Manhattan, although the atmosphere is reminiscent of a busy station bar.
210 E 46th Street, Second
and Third Avenue,
Tel 212-687-48 55,
Mon–Thurs 12.00–23.00,
Fri 12.00–23.30, Sat 17.00–
23.30.

ACCOMMODATION

Algonquin Hotel Famous hotel in the Theater District and one of the city's most illustrious hotels since 1902.
59 West 44th Street
(near Sixth Avenue),
Tel 212-840-68 00,
www.algonquinhotel.com

Casablanca Hotel The lobby will transport you onto the set

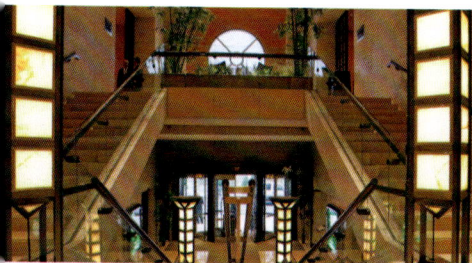

The lobby of the Four Seasons Hotel alone shows why the legendry hotel regularly features in the best-of lists.

of the famous movie. The rooms are luxuriously appointed; the tearoom is called "Rick's Café".
*147 West 43rd Street (near Broadway),
Tel 212-869-12 12,
www.casablancahotel.com*

Four Seasons Hotel Stars like Marilyn Monroe have stayed in this legendary, luxury hotel, one of the best and most famous in the world.
*57 East 57th Street (near Park Avenue),
Tel 212-758-57 00,
www.fourseasons.com*

Millennium Broadway This elegant art deco hotel is situated in Theater land only two blocks from Times Square and as many extras.
*45 West 44th Street (near Sixth Avenue),
Tel 212-768-44 00,
www.millenniumhotels.com.*

Le Parker Meridien Apart from an excellent restaurant, this hotel other extras, such as ergonomically designed chairs. The speedy lifts have cartoons playing on built-in TV screens.
*118 West 57th Street (near Sixth Avenue,
Tel 212-245-50 00,
www.parkermeridien.com*

Salisbury Hotel This simple hotel is situated opposite Carnegie Hall. The rooms are quite large for such a budget price hotel. A few dollars will buy you the continental breakfast.
*123 West 57th Street,
Tel 212-246-13 00,
www.nycsalisbury.com*

Sofitel The rooms here are small, but the art deco surroundings make up for it. Best rooms are on the upper floor
*45 West 44th Street
Tel 212-354-884,
www.sofitel.com*

NIGHTLIFE

Failte Irish Whiskey Bar An Irish pub as it should be: warm yourself at the fire, with Guinness and whiskey.
*531 Second Avenue (near 30th Street),
Tel 212-725-94 40,
12.00–4.00, daily.*

Marquee To get past the heavy bouncers you need to be "young and beautiful". *289 Tenth Avenue (near 26th Street),
Tel 646-473-02 02,
www.marqueeny.com,
Tues 22.00–4.00, Wed–Sat 22.30–4.00*

Niagara A retro bar, reminiscent of old New York: the speakers pump out dance tracks from the last 30 years.
*112 Avenue A (corner Seventh Street), Tel 212-420-95 17, www.niagarabar.com,
16.00–4.00, daily.*

The arts and crafts and design collection of the Cooper Hewitt Museum comprises both historical and contemporary items.

MUSEUMS, MUSIC, DRAMA

Asia Society Museum The museum has a significant collection of East Asiatic art and cultural objects from the 11th to the 19th centuries, most of which were once owned by magnate John D Rockefeller III; it also specializes in modern Asiatic and American-Asian art. Changing exhibitions, lectures, dance performances, concerts, and film screenings complete the schedule.
725 Park Avenue/70th Street,
Tel 212-288-64 00,
www.asiasociety.org,
Tues–Sun 11.00–18.00,
Fri 11.00–21.00.

Cooper Hewitt Museum (National Museum of Design) The museum is housed in the old townhouse of Andrew Carnegie, the steel king. Here the Smithsonian Institution shows in changing exhibitions one of the world's largest design and crafts collections. The core of the collection was amassed by sisters Sarah, Eleanor, and Amy Hewitt, granddaughters of the steel magnate Peter Cooper, before 1897.
91st Street/Fifth Avenue,
Tel 212-849-84 00,
www.cooperhewitt.org,
Mon–Fri 10.00–17.00,
Sat 10.00–18.00, Sun 12.00–18.00.

Delacorte Theater Every summer since 1962, Shakespeare in the Park Productions has been performing free plays by Shakespeare, on its open-air stage in Central Park.
Mid-Park, Central Park West,
81st Street,
Tel 212-861-72 77,
www.centralpark.com

El Museo del Barrio Founded in 1969 and New York's leading Latino cultural institution and community place, the museum exhibits Latino, Caribbean, and Latin American art and culture from pre-Columbian cultures to the present day.
1230 Fifth Avenue,
Tel 212-831-72 72,
www.elmuseo.org

Mount Vernon Hotel Museum (formerly the Abigail Adams Smith Museum) A legendary museum based in a hotel, located in a 1799 carriage house since 1826, and once a secluded retreat for stressed-out New Yorkers back in the day when the city only reached as far as 14th Street. One of the seven oldest buildings in Manhattan, the original furniture and fixtures here give a good idea of every-day life in the period.
421 East 61st Street,
Tel 212-838-68 78,
www.mvhm.org,
Tues–Sun 11.00–16.00.

Getrude Vanderbilt Whitney founded the Whitney Museum of American Art to help promote contemporary American art.

Museum of American Illustration (Society of Illustrators) Founded in 1901, the society promotes the work of illustrators and its gallery has a collection of more than 2,000 original works by famous American illustrators.
128 East 63rd Street,
Tel 212-838-25 60,
www.societyillustrators.org,
Tues 10.00–20.00, Wed–Fri
10.00–17.00, Sat 12.00– 16.00.

Museum of the City of New York This is the place to witness an overview of the city's three-hundred-year history and its development from discovery through the settlement of Nieuw Amsterdam to the present day, looking at lifestyles from other periods, the city's cultural life, and even old toys.
1220 Fifth Avenue/103rd
Street, Tel 212-534-16 72,
www.mcny.org,
Tues–Sun 10.00–17.00.

Neue Galerie New York Housed since 1994 in a neo-classical building on the Museum Mile, the collection, which partly belongs to Ronald S Lauder, heir to the cosmetics firm, exhibits Austrian art from the turn of the 20th century, including Gustav Klimt's iconic Adele Bloch-Bauer and some works by German expressionists. Lauder, a former American ambassador to Austria, was much involved in the restitution of stolen Jewish art.
1048 Fifth Avenue,
Tel 212-628-62 00,
www.neuegalerie.org,
Thurs–Mon 11.00–18.00.

The Jewish Museum Founded in 1904, the Museum owns one of the largest collections of Jewish documents worldwide, spanning some 4,000 years of Jewish history.
1109 Fifth Avenue/92nd
Street, Tel 212-423-32 00,
www.thejewishmuseum.org,
Sun–Tues, Thurs, Sat 11.00–
17.45, Fri 11.00–16.00/17.45.

Whitney Museum of American Art The most important collection of 20th-century American art is located in a building designed by Marcel Breuer. The museum holds works by the Ashcan School, Alexander Calder, Keith Haring, Edward Hopper, Jasper Johns, Franz Kline, Edward Kienholz, Willem de Kooning, Jackson Pollock, George Segal, and Cindy Sherman, among others. It was founded in 1931 by the heiress, and artist, Gertrude Vanderbilt to promote modern American art. Philip Morris Park has a Whitney branch with a sculpture garden.
945 Madison Avenue/
75th Street, Tel 212-570-36 00,
www.whitney.org,
Wed–Thurs 11.00–18.00,
13.00–21.00, Sat–Sun 11.00–
18.00.

If you're in New York on Thanksgiving Day, make sure you don't miss the fun and cheer during Macy's Thanksgiving Day Parade.

FESTIVALS AND EVENTS

Central Park Summerstage This summer festival offers a variety of different and interesting cultural events: music, dance, film, and readings by famous artists. Many of the events are free, some ask for a small donation, and others are ticketed.
www.summerstage.org, Jun–Aug

Macy's Thanksgiving Day Parade New York's biggest department store puts on this gigantic show for young and old alike on Thanksgiving Day. Brightly painted floats, marching bands, cheerleaders, and troupes of clowns and dancers all make for a happy atmosphere, but the parade is most famous for its giant inflatable celebrated comic or toy characters. The last float is occupied by Macy's Santa Claus.
From the Museum of Natural History (Central Park) via Broadway to Herald Square, www.macys.com, fourth Thurs in Nov, from 9.00.

Philharmonic in the Park In the summertime, the famous New York Philharmonic gives free evening concerts at various locations in every borough. There are open-air events in Central Park, Prospect Park in Brooklyn and in parks in Queens, the Bronx, Staten Island, and other districts.
Tel 212-875-56 56, http://nyphil.org, July.

Shakespeare in the Park In the summer the Delacorte Theater is given over to Shakespeare, with actors performing for free. Get tickets early on the day of the performance.
www.publictheater.org, Jun–Aug, performances begin at 20.30.

Steuben Day Parade This German-American parade attracts thousands of spectators who cheer on the brightly painted floats, groups in traditional folk costume, choirs, dancing troupes, marching bands, dignitaries, and lots of cultural societies. The spectacle has been held since 1957 to commemorate the Prussian general von Steuben, a hero of the American War of Independence, and the arrival of the first German settlers in 1683.
Fifth Avenue from East 63rd–86th Street, www.germanparadenyc.org, third weekend in Sep.

SPORT, GAMES, FUN

Jogging Central Park, not to mention the many other parks in the city, is a haven for joggers. The huge number of wide paths in the parks are especially suited for running during the

HIre your boat from Loeb Boathouse and row it gently across the lake – a welcome contrast to the bustle of hektic Manhattan.

periods when cars are banned, although you will also be sharing the park with cyclists, skate-boarders and skaters.
New York Road Runners Club, Tel 212-860-44 55, www.nyrrc.org, Car-free periods: Mon–Fri 10.00–15.00, 19.00–7.00, Sat, Sun 24 hours.

Loeb Boathouse If the weather is warm and sunny, you can hire rowing boats here and explore the beautiful Central Park Lake. If you prefer the luxury of someone else doing the rowing, you can always hire a gondola with a gondolier. The attractive restaurant has excellent views of both the Park and the city.
Park Drive North/East 72nd Street, Tel 212-517-22 33, www.thecentralpark boathouse.com, Apr–end of Oct, 9.30–17.30 (depending on weather).

HEALTH AND BEAUTY

Asphalt Green You can learn the butterfly stroke or other swimming styles in the pool of this not-for-profit organization, and the trainer will watch your technique through windows in the pool wall. The smaller pools have other programs and there are many courses for children. The sports and fitness schedule is pretty comprehensive with a range of activities for everyone.
555 East 90th Street/York Avenue, Tel 212-369-88 90, www.asphaltgreen.org, Mon–Fri 5.30–22.00, Sat–Sun 8.00–20.00.

Paul Labrecque East This is a beauty salon for stars and those who want to be seen with them. If you wish to be attended to by Mr Paul, the owner, himself you will have to pay a little more.

171 East 65th Street/Lexington Avenue, Tel 212-988-78 16, www.paullabrecque.com, Mon–Fri 8.00–21.00, Sat 9.00–20.00, Sun 10.00–20.00.

SHOPPING

Calvin Klein The cult designer's biggest store in New York has four floors of clothes, shoes, and household goods. Shop till you drop.
654 Madison Avenue/ East 60th Street, Tel 212-292-90 00, www.calvinklein.com, Mon–Wed, Fri–Sat 10.00–18.00, Thurs 10.00–19.00, Sun 12.00–18.00.

Donna Karan New York (DKNY) Donna Karan's flagship store is a small, very friendly establishment selling fashion (especially women's clothes) and accessories by the famous designer.

A visit to Sotheby's is worth it even if you don't intend to bid.

819 Madison Avenue/
East 69th Street,
www.donnakaran.com,
Mon–Wed, Fri–Sat 10.00–
18.00, Thurs 10.00–19.00,
Sun 12.00–17.00.

Little Shop of Crafts New York's largest store for crafts equipment. You can buy materials for your projects here – then get creative in their crafts workshop.
431 East 73rd Street,
Tel 212-717-66 36,
www.littleshopny.com,
Mon–Tues 11.00–18.30, Wed–
Fri 11.00–22.00, Sat 10.00–
20.00, Sun 10.00–18.30.

Sotheby's Just as at Christie's there are almost daily auctions of antiques, art objects, carpets, jewels, coins, books, and more. Drop in and watch even if you don't want to bid.
1334 York Avenue./East 72nd
Street, Tel 212-606-70 00,

www.sothebys.com,
Mon–Sat 10.00–17.00, Sun
12.00–17.00, mid-Jul to early
Sep: closed Sat, Sun.

EATING AND DRINKING

Accademia di Vino Two bars located in a pleasant restaurant. Kevin Garcia, the head chef, offers a wide range of Italian dishes, including good pizzas, salads, and antipasti. There are more than 500 bottles in the wine cellar.
1081 Third Avenue
(near 64th Street),
Tel 212-888-63 33,
www.accademiadivino.com,
12.00–24.00, daily.

Barking Dog A dog-oriented bar – there is even a "doggie bar" with water bowls near the entrance for (wo)man's best friend. Two-legged guests will enjoy the good breakfasts and classics such as meatloaf.

1678 Third Avenue
(corner 94th Street),
Tel 212-831-18 00,
8.00–23.00, daily.

Beyoglu A very friendly Turkish bar, which has been described by some critics as "the best Turkish restaurant in the city". The doner kebab is made from the best meat and all the specials are very inviting, especially the fish dishes which are made with fresh herbs.
1431 Third Avenue
(corner 81st Street),
Tel 212-650-08 50,
12.00–23.30, daily.

California Pizza Kitchen Originally founded in California in 1985, this restaurant chain has since spread right across the United States. Crispy pizzas with quirky toppings such as Peking duck or spicy curry are a trademark of this successful fast food outlet.

CENTRAL PARK AND UPPER EAST SIDE

Mediterranean delicacies are on the menu of Fig & Olive. The adjacent store also has a great selection of wines.

201 East 60th Street,
Tel 212-755-77 73,
www.cpk.com,
Sun–Thurs 11.30–22.00,
Fri, Sat 11.30–23.00.

40 Carrots The girls from *Sex and the City* might just have dropped by; the frozen yogurt is low in calories and refreshing after a hard day's shopping.
1000 Third Avenue, (Bloomingdale's, basement),
Tel 212-705-30 85
Mon–Fri 10.00–19.00,
Sat, Sun 10.00–18.00.

Centolire A rustic atmosphere somewhat reminiscent of a trattoria in Tuscany. Pino Luongo, the head chef, serves up authentic Italian cuisine, particularly from Tuscany and northern Italy.
1167 Madison Avenue (near 86th Street),
Tel 212-734-77 11,
Mon–Sat 12.00–15.00, 17.30–

22.30, Sun 11.30–15.00,
17.00–21.00.

Cinema Brasserie The posters and pictures on the walls here recall such legendary films as *Casablanca*. There is "cinema popcorn" on the menu, of course, but this little restaurant also serves delicious sandwiches, wraps, as well as crispy-based pizza.
45 East 60th Street
(near Madison Avenue),
Tel 212-750-75 00,
www.cinemarestaurants.com,
Mon–Fri 11.00–22.00,
Sat 9.00–21.00,
Sun 10.00–18.00.

David Burke Townhouse Located in an unassuming townhouse, David Burke's restaurant is renowned principally for its original and elaborate presentation. It has won a prize for being the best lobster restaurant, and the salmon

and tuna parfaits and the delicious dessert, butterscotch panna cotta are also tipped for awards.
133 East 61st Street (near Lexington Avenue),
Tel 212-813-21 21,
www.dbdrestaurant.com,
Mon–Fri 11.45–14.30, 17.00–23.00, Sat 12.00–14.30,
17.00–23.00, Sun 11.00–14.30,
16.30–21.00.

Delmonico Gourmet A characterful lunch bar on the Upper East Side; most of the lunchtime regulars take their meals "to go", usually pasta and seafood salads, Chinese and Japanese fare, steamed vegetables with a selection of exotic dressings, and of course every variety of sandwich filling you can possibly imagine.
55 East 59th Street (near Madison Avenue),
Tel 212-751-55 59,
open 24/7.

Many restaurants serve delicious sushi – fresh and often in a stunning presentation.

Fig & Olive Mediterranean charm on the Upper East Side. Side. As the name suggests, good quality olive oil is added to almost every dish; try the fig and olive salad.
808 Lexington Avenue (near 62nd Street),
Tel 212-207-45 55,
www.figandolive.com,
11.00–23.00, daily.

Gajyumaru A tiny sushi bar, and one of the best on the Upper East Side. The toro (tuna) and the uni (sea urchin) are the best dishes.
1659 First Avenue
(near 87th Street),
Tel 212-860-88 57,
Tues–Sat 12.00–14.30, 17.00–23.00, Sun 12.00–14.30, 17.00–22.30.

Hokkaido Sushi An excellent sushi bar, which sets great store by design. The Manhattan rolls (with tempura shrimp)

and the spicy tuna are arranged to resemble the New York skyline. The sushi is of above average quality and your choice is best left to the sushi chef.
1817 Second Avenue
(corner 94th Street),
Tel 212-289-19 02,
www.hokkaidosushi.com,
Mon–Sat 11.00–15.00, 17.00–23.30, Sun 13.00–23.30.

I Vandali The friendly waiters give you sticks of chalk and ask you to "vandalize" the walls by brightening them up with graffiti. It's only a clever gimmick, as the food is well-worthcoming for. Marco Sanmartino, the head chef, serves up first-class antipasti and creative pasta dishes.
1590 First Avenue
(near 83rd Street),
Tel 212-585-33 39,
www.ivandalinyc.com,
Sun–Thurs 17.00–23.00, Fri, Sat 17.00–23.30.

Le Refuge Authentic French cuisine served up in a small restaurant with a generally older clientele. The filet of beef melts in the mouth, and the house specials worth trying include duck with green beans and almonds, and the lamb ratatouille.
166 East 82nd Street (near Lexington Avenue),
Tel 212-861-45 05,
www.lerefugenyc.com,
17.00–23.00, daily.

Le Train Bleu A top tip for Bloomingdale's customers: next to the household goods section you'll find a pleasant little bar located in a recreated 1920s railway carriage (named after the famous Parisian restaurant) – your shopping goes in the luggage rack. The food is excellent and eclectic with delicacies like pheasant pâté with Cumberland sauce and Japanese soba noodles.

The Orsay is a typical French bistro just like you'd you expect to see in Paris.

1000 Third Avenue (corner 59th Street), Tel 212-705-21 00, Mon–Wed, Fri, Sat 10.30–17.00, Thurs 10.30–19.00, Sun 10.30–16.30.

Maya Maya is one of the best and most up-to-date Mexican restaurants in town. Richard Sandoval, the owner, serves traditional Mexican food minus the traditional Tex-Mex additions you usually find in the United States.

1191 First Avenue (near 64th Street), Tel 212-585-18 18, www.modernmexican.com, Sun–Thurs 17.00–22.00, Fri, Sat 17.00–23.00.

Mustang Grill Mexican food lovers are looked after in this little cantina until late into the night. The house specials include quesadilla and spicy chicken with jalapeños, but most people come here for the excellent margaritas.

1633 Second Avenue (corner 85th Street), Tel 212-744-91 94, www.mustanggrill.com, Mon–Wed 11.30–1.00, Thurs Fri 11.30–3.00, Sat 10.00–3.00, Sun 10.00–1.00.

Nica Trattoria A Sicilian trattoria with an authentic family atmosphere. The owners swear by fresh ingredients and their first-class gnocchi with various sauces is excellent. The classic pasta dishes are also highly recommended.

354 East 84th Street (near First Avenue), Tel 212-472-50 40, www.nica-nyc.com, 17.30–22.30, daily.

Orsay It feels like you're dining in Paris in this delightful French bistro. The atmosphere seems authentic even if the waiters don't speak any French, and the appetizers, particularly the lobster salad and the smoked salmon are an excellent treat for the palate.

1057 Lexington Avenue (corner 75th Street), Tel 212-517-64 00, www.orsayrestaurant.com, Mon–Fri 12.00–15.00, 17.30–23.00, Sat 12.00–15.30, 17.30–23.00, Sun 11.00–15.30, 17.30–2.00.

Parlor Steakhouse One of the city's newest and best steakhouses. The quality of the steaks is high, particularly the filet mignon, and the fish dishes are tender, fresh and also well spiced.

1600 Third Avenue (corner 90th Street), Tel 212-423-58 88, www.parlorsteakhouse.com, Mon–Thurs 11.45–23.00, Fri 11.45–24.00, Sat 11.00–24.00, Sun 11.00–22.00.

Chef and owner Kenji Takahashi fileting a fish for his top-quality sushi.

Peri Ela Don't be put off by the gloomy drawing-room atmosphere; Peri Ela is one of the few restaurants in New York with authentic Turkish food, as guaranteed by the owners, Silay and Jill Ciner and their family.
1361 Lexington Avenue (near 90th Street),
Tel 212-410-43 00, 12.00–16.00, 17.00–23.00, daily.

Pio Pio Much more than fast food: the grilled chicken in this popular little Peruvian bar have got very little to do with KFC and the other well-known chicken chains. Before the meat is placed on the grill at Pio Pio, it is marinated in Peruvian beer and other (highly secret) ingredients to give the dish the right kick.
1746 First Avenue (near 90th Street),
Tel 212-426-58 00, 11.00–23.00, daily.

Primola A relaxed lounge ambience in one of the most popular Italian restaurants on the Upper East Side. Giuliano Zuliani swears by fine Italian cooking and his fish and mussel dishes are particularly popular choices
1226 Second Avenue (near 64th Street),
Tel 212-758-17 75,
Mon–Fri 12.00–15.00, 17.00–23.00, Sat, Sun 17.00–23.00.

Sala Thai An unassuming Thai restaurant located on the Upper East Side; it's nothing special on the ouside, but inside has very good curry dishes. The vegetables are fresh and crunchy, the rice is well cooked and the sauces always piping hot and spicy.
1718 Second Avenue (near 89th Street),
Tel 212-410-55 57,
Mon–Sat 17.00–23.00, Sun 17.00–22.30.

Sasabune "Today's special – trust me" boasts the menu, and you can put your faith in Kenji Takahashi, the sushi chef here. The tasting menu uses only the finest raw fish and features such creative starters as salmon wrapped in seaweed and albacore sashimi with ponzu sauce. The fish simply melts in the mouth. Easily the best sushi bar in north Manhattan.
401 East 73rd Street (near First Avenue),
Tel 212-249-85 83,
Tues–Fri 12.00–14.00, 17.30–22.00, Sat 17.30–22.00.

Sfoglia It's just like eating with a real Italian family – there are only ten tables in this tiny but respectable Italian restaurant. The theme here is delicious, pepped-up but authentic Italian home cooking.
1402 Lexington Avenue (corner 92nd Street),

Spare ribs and BBQ Chicken – Southern style hospitality with a taste of St Louis or Memphis!

Tel 212-831-14 02,
www.sfogliarestaurant.com,
Mon 17.30–22.30, Tues–Sat
12.00–14.30, 17.30–22.30.

Shanghai Pavilion It's not just Chinatown that boasts first-class Chinese restaurants. The Shanghai Pavilion on the Upper East Side has a surprisingly authentic selection of first-class dishes.
1378 Third Avenue
(near 78th Street),
Tel 212-585-33 88,
Mon–Fri 11.30–22.30,
Sat, Sun 12.00–22.30.

Slice, the Perfect Food It's not just the vegetarians who swear by this pizza restaurant on the Upper East Side. Only organic vegetables and free-range beef is used on the crispy pizza bases.
1413 Second Avenue
(near 74th Street),
Tel 212-249-43 53,

www.sliceperfect.com,
Mon–Wed 11.00–22.00,
Thurs–Sun 11.00–23.00.

Southern Hospitality Justin Timberlake, the co-owner, attracts a few fans, but most of the patrons come here because of the hearty spare ribs and the BBQ chicken. Have fries, beans, and biscuits with them.
1460 Second Avenue
(near 76th Street),
Tel 212-249-10 01,
www.southern
hospitalitybbq.com
Mon–Fri 16.00–2.00,
Sat, Sun 11.30–2.00.

Swifty's A somewhat loud and rather uncomfortable restaurant, but that doesn't seem to bother any of the diners here. The tasty food makes up for everything; they serve traditional New England specialties.
1007 Lexington Avenue (
near 72nd Street),

Tel 212-535-60 00,
www.swiftysnyc.com,
Mon–Fri 12.00–15.30, 17.30–
23.15, Sat, Sun 12.00– 16.00,
17.30–23.15.

Taco Taco Regulars swear by the margaritas and the guacamole here. The tacos, always made with fresh ingredients and first-class meat, are also excellent. The pork is marinated in a tasty jalapeño sauce and is as wonderfully hot.
1726 Second Avenue
(near 90th Street),
Tel 212-289-82 26,
Sun–Thurs 11.30–23.00,
Fri, Sat 11.30–24.00.

Tiramisu The tiramisu tastes good here, of course, but the thin-crust oven pizza and the pasta dishes are also recommended, including ravioli alla Cardinale, ricotta and spinach ravioli with shrimps, and zucchini in tomato sauce.

One of the luxurious suites at the Loews Regency Hotel. Of course it doesn't come cheap …

1410 Third Avenue (corner 80th Street), Tel 212-988-97 80, 12.00–23.30, daily.

Viand This diner, which opened in 1976, has always been a good place to stop off after a shopping trip. The turkey sandwich is legendary.
673 Madison Avenue (corner 61st Street), Tel 212-751-66 22, 6.00–22.00, daily

Zebú Grill The caipirinhas are delicious in this first-class Brazilian restaurant, one of the few located in Manhattan, but that's not all. The mixed grill with South American spicy meat is a winner.
305 East 92nd Street (near Second Avenue), Tel 212-426-75 00, www.zebugrill.com, Mon–Sat 17.00–23.30, Sun 16.30–22.00.

ACCOMMODATION

Affinia Gardens The junior suites in this "all-suites" hotel located on the Upper East Side are all equipped with a kitchen. The décor is simple with a warm atmosphere.
215 East 64th Street (near Third Avenue), Tel 212-355-12 30, www.affinia.com

Hotel Wales The rooms in this lovingly decorated hotel give it a homely atmosphere; the gym and the business facilities are modern. The continental breakfast is included in the price.
1295 Madison Avenue (near 92nd Street), Tel 212-876-60 00, www.waleshotel.com

Loews Regency Hotel Elegant and expensive, like all the hotels on the Upper East Side, the Regency now has a regal gloss after a program of extensive renovations. Valuable mahogany furniture and luxurious fabrics in the rooms give it a timeless elegance. Unusually for a top-end hotel, provisions are made for pets.
540 Park Avenue (corner 61st Street), Tel 212-759-41 00, www.loewshotels.com

The Carlyle Named after the British essayist Thomas Carlyle, this hotel has been one of the finest on the Upper East Side since the 1930s. A timeless classic, the spacious rooms resemble private apartments and feature lots of extras. A sophisticated place to stay.
35 East 76th Street (corner Madison Avenue), Tel 212-744-16 00, www.thecarlyle.com

The Franklin Hotel The rooms in this hotel recall the 1950s, and some are pretty small.

The Carlyle: an elegant hotel, not just for VIPs.

There are extras, however – wireless Internet access, plasma TVsandnewspapers. A European breakfast is inclusive.
164 East 87th Street
(near Lexington Avenue),
Tel 212-369-10 00,
www.franklinhotel.com

The Helmsley Carlton House
A first-class hotel with an inviting lobby, bright, spacious rooms, and attentive service.
680 Madison Avenue
(corner 61st Street),
Tel 212-838-30 00,
http://helmsleyhotels.com

The Lowell You can't get a room in this elegant hotel for under $500 but you can at least see where your money is going – the spacious rooms are furnished with the finest carpets and fabrics and the service is exceptional – the staff will even shop for you.
28 East 63rd Street

(corner Madison Avenue),
Tel 212-838-14 00,
www.lowellhotel.com

NIGHTLIFE

Bailey's Corner Pub This Irish pub has been the first choice for Upper East Side night owls since 1951. The counter top was originally part of a 19th-century tavern.
1607 York Avenue
(corner 85th Street),
Tel 212-650-13 41,
Mon–Sat 11.00–4.00,
Sun 12.00–4.00.

Club Macanudo Smoking is allowed in only a few clubs in the city; this one has the best atmosphere.
26 East 63rd Street (corner Madison Avenue),
Tel 212-752-82 00,
www.clubmacanudonyc.com,
Mon, Tues 17.00–1.00,
Wed–Sat 17.00-1.30.

Iggy's Karaoke Bar & Grill
Singing and Irish beer in by far the best NYC karaoke bar.
1452 Second Avenue
(near 76th Street),
Tel 212-327-30 43,
www.iggysnewyork.com,
12.00–4.00, daily.

Saloon Not a glitzy spot to go and be seen in – this place is for serious dancers. The clientele, generally in their twenties, strut their stuff on the dance floor to top 40 hits.
1584 York Avenue
(near 84th Street),
Tel 212 570-54 54,
www.saloonnyc.com

Vudu Lounge The giant mirror ball, the dry ice, and go-go girlson skimp skirts are reminiscent of a 70s disco.
1487 First Avenue
(near 78th Street),
Tel 212-249-95 40,
www.vudulounge.com

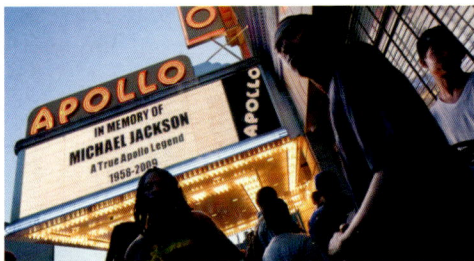

The Apollo Theater is the stuff of legends as a concert venue where Duke Ellington and Louis Armstrong once appeared.

MUSEUMS, MUSIC, DRAMA

Apollo Theater Since opening in 1913, the legendary Apollo Theater has had a tumultuous history, including the banning of black patrons in 1934, a temporary conversion into a cinema, closure in 1976, reopening in 1985, and above all the Amateur Night shows, which led to the discovery of such talents as Ella Fitzgerald, Billie Holiday, and Michael Jackson.
253 West 125th Street,
Tel 212-531-53 00,
www.apollotheater.org,
Tours Mon–Fri 11.00, 13.00,
15.00 (except Thurs only
11.00), Sat, Sun 11.00, 13.00.

Children's Museum of Manhattan Founded in 1973 and famed for its wide variety of very informative and entertaining activities, from fascinating scientific experiments to puppet plays and an introduction to a television studio. The museum is also a useful source of ideas for teachers.
212 West 83rd Street,
Tel 212-721-12 34,
www.cmom.org,
Tues–Sun 10.00–17.00.

David H. Koch Theater (formerly New York State Theater) Built by Philip Johnson and Richard Foster in the Lincoln Center in 1964, this building is now the home of the New York City Opera Company and the New York City Ballet.
Lincoln Center, Broadway/
64th Street,
Tel 212-870-55 70,
www.lincolncenter.org

Dyckman Farmhouse Museum Dating back to 1784 and with its original furnishings, the only remaining old farmhouse in Manhattan was made accessible to the public as a museum in 1916.

4881 Broadway/204th Street,
Tel 212-304-94 22,
www.dyckmanfarmhouse.org,
Wed–Sat 11.00–16.00,
Sun 12.00–16.00.

Hispanic Society Museum Fascinating archaeological finds, craft pieces, sculptures, and paintings from Spain, Portugal, and South America are the core of the collection, which has works by El Greco, Velazquez, Zurbaràn, Ribera, Murillo, and Goya.
Audubon Terrace, Broadway,
Tel 212-926-22 34,
www.hispanicsociety.org,
Tues–Sat 10.00–16.30,
Sun 13.00–16.00.

Lincoln Center Plaza Graced with a fountain by Philip Johnson, in August the middle of the Lincoln Center becomes a venue for street theater and other free performance.
Lincoln Center, Broadway.

Almost all the famous composers from the late 19th century onward have had their work performed at the Metropolitan Opera, or Met.

Metropolitan Opera (Met) Built to a design by Wallace K. Harrison in 1966, the opera house is the architectural heart of the Lincoln Center for the Performing Arts. In the foyer behind the high arcades there are two large murals by Marc Chagall, the *Sources of Music* in yellow and the *Triumph of Music* in red, and three bronzes by Aristide Maillol. The corridors are decorated with portraits of famous opera singers. One of the world's leading opera houses, the Met is also the home of the Metropolitan Opera Company and the American Ballet Theater since 1880. Enrico Caruso, Maria Callas, Arturo Toscanini, and Gustav Mahler have all appeared here. *Lincoln Center, Broadway/ 64th Street, Tel 212-362-60 00, www.metoperafamily.org, information for all events and the start of all guided tours are in the lower floor.*

Morris-Jumel Mansion Museum This Palladian country house, built in 1765 and once belonging to an English family, is one of the oldest houses in Manhattan, and was used by George Washington as his headquarters in 1776 during the American War of Independence. The Mansion has also been host to British military leaders. A museum of American history opened in 1904. *65 Jumel Terrace, Tel 212-923-80 08, www.risjumel.org, Wed–Sun 10.00–16.00.*

Nitchen Children's Museum of Native America Located in an old church building, this museum offers plenty of fun activities for children to help illustrate the history of America's indigenous peoples. *550W 155th Street, Tel 212-694-22 40, www.nitchenchildrens*

museum.org, Mon–Fri 8.00–14.00.

Schomburg Center for Research in Black Culture This research organization for black art, culture, and history is the largest of its type in in the world.The reading rooms and archives offer an insight into black history and culture. *515 Malcom X Boulevard Tel 212-491-42200, www.nypl.org/research/sc, Mon–Wed 12.00–20.00, Thurs, Fri 11.00–18.00, Sat 10.00–17.00.*

Studio Museum Harlem Set up in 1970, the museum holds temporary exhibitions of contemporary Afro-American art, literature, and music. *144 West 125th Street, Tel 212-864-45 00, www.studiomuseum.org, Wed–Fri 10.00–17.00, Sat, Sun 13.00–18.00.*

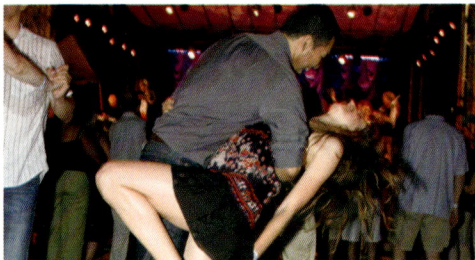

From blues to swing, from salsa to tango, from soul to funk – the motto of the Midsummer Night Swing is dance all night.

New York Historical Society Museum Founded as a scientific institution with a large library in 1809, the museum offers an interesting overview of the history of both the city and of America.
170 Central Park West/77th Street, Tel 212-873-34 00, www.nyhistory.org, Tues–Thurs, Sat 10.00–18.00, Fri 10.00–20.00, Sun 11.00–17.45.

FESTIVALS AND EVENTS

Blessing of the Animals Many pet-owners bring their charges to the Cathedral of St John the Divine to have them blessed on the feast of St Francis. Recordings of whales, birdsong, and wolves howling are played to the accompaniment of a human choir during the church service.
1057 Amsterdam Avenue/ 112th Street,

Tel 212-316-75 40, www.stjohndivine.org, beginning of Oct, tickets from 9.00, service from 11.00.

Harlem Week This summer festival features a street festival with numerous market stalls and all sorts of tasty snacks (especially soul food) on sale, as well as concerts (jazz, soul, funk, and modern), cabaret, and sports events for all the family.
www.harlemdiscover.com, end of Jul–Sept.

Midsummer Night Swing "New York's biggest outdoor dance party" sees hundreds of enthusiasts dancing until late into the night.
Josie Robertson Plaza in the Lincoln Center, Columbus Avenue/West 64th–66th Street, Tel 212-875-54 56, http://new.lincolncenter.org, Jun–Jul.

New York Film Festival At the annual New York Film Festival the best and the most recent films from the United States and abroad are presented at the Alice Tully Hall in the Lincoln Center .
Columbus Avenue/West 64th–66th St, Tel 212-875-54 56, www.new.lincolncenter.org and www.filminc.com, end of Sept–mid-Oct.

SPORT, GAMES, FUN

Harlem Spirituals Tours This agency runs a selection of guided tours to Harlem, visiting places that have hitherto been off the beaten tourist track, such as Duke Ellington's house and the city's oldest black parish, the Mother African Methodist Episcopal Zion Church, where Sunday services are always accompanied by gospel choir music. They also run evening and jazz tours.

Why not explore the city on roller-blades? Central Park has beautiful paths where you'll find many enthusiasts.

590 Eighth Avenue/West
43rd–44th Street,
Tel 212-391-09 00,
www.harlemspirituals.com

Blades, Board & Skates Not far from Central Park on the Upper West Side, Blades, Board & Skates hires out rollerblades throughout the year. There are several areas in the city dedicated to rollerblading, such as in Central Park near the Naumberg Bandshell (freestyle).
156 West 72nd Street,
Tel 212-787-39 11,
www.blades.com,
Mon–Sat 10.00–20.00,
Sun–19.00.

HEALTH AND BEAUTY

Spa in Mandarin Oriental If money isn't a problem, don't miss the five-star spa and gym which is spread over several floors of this luxury hotel. You can relax in the pool or the Thai yoga suite, or even in the separate very luxurious VIP spa suite, which has its very own fireplace.
80 Columbus Circle/60th
Street, Tel 212-805-88 00,
www.mandarinoriental.com,
9.00–21.00, daily.

SHOPPING

Atmos The futuristic decoration and lighting make this store look like a spaceship and it sells the trendy goods you might expect in such surroundings: trainers of the most garish shades and patterns, crazy one-off t-shirts with wicked logos that you won't find anywhere else. Even firms like Levi's and New Balance test the market's tastes with few quirky lines here, and a lot of the fashion comes from young, Japanese designers.
203 W 125th Street,
Tel 212-666-22 42,
Mon–Sat 11.00–20.00,
Sun 12.00–19.00.

Harlemade A relaxed atmosphere in which to buy clothes, jewelry, and craft items from the Harlem designer label. You will also find souvenirs of Harlem with the Harlemade emblem.
174 Malcolm X Blvd./
West 118th Street,
Tel 212-987-25 00,
Mon–Fri 11.30–19.00,
Sat 11.00–19.00,
Sun 12.00–18.00.

Harlem's Heaven Hat Boutique Anyone who has admired the adventurous millinery of Afro-American ladies and gentlemen will find it for sale here, as well as accessories.
2538 Adam Clayton Powell Jr.
Boulevard/West 147th Street,
Tel 212-491-77 06,
www.harlemsheaven.com,
Tues–Sat 12.00–18.00.

The superb French goods for sale at the Boucheron Bakery are worth a fortune – but no good for those on a diet.

Nicholas A shop to really put a backbeat in the pulse of every reggae fan; you can buy printed t-shirts, jackets, belts, caps, scarves, and bags displaying the image of the legendary Jamaican musician Bob Marley.
2035 Fifth Avenue/125th Street, Tel 212-289-36 28, www.wholesalecentral.com/ nicholasvariety, Mon–Sat 9.00–20.00, Sun 12.00–18.00.

Whole Foods New York's biggest supermarket (and self-service restaurant) is located here in the basement of the Time Warner Building and has an overwhelming selection of fresh produce (including organic foods).
10 Columbus Circle, Tel 212-823-96 00, www.wholefoodsmarket.com, 8.00–23.00, daily, restricted opening times on public hols.

EATING AND DRINKING

Amy Ruth's Home-Style Southern Cuisine Possibly the best soul food in Harlem, with hearty homemade Southern-style food. The fried and BBQ chicken is served with potato purée, baked beans, or buttered corn, and the macaroni cheese is very popular.
113 West 116th Street, Tel 212-280-87 79, www.amyruthsharlem.com, Mon 11.30–23.00, Tues–Thurs 8.30–23.00, Fri 8.30–5.30, Sat 7.30–5.30, Sun 7.30–23.00.

Bouchon Bakery A hint of France in the middle of New York: Thomas Keller's boulangerie serves tasty quiches and soups as well as croissants, rolls, cakes, and other treats.
10 Columbus Circle (2nd floor), Tel 212-823-93 66, Mon–Fri 8.00–21.00, Sat 10.00–21.00, Sun 10.00–19.00.

Key West Diner One of the most popular diners in New York since 1987. Giant burgers, omelets, and salads are popular with regulars – and even the coffee is recommended, too. The Greek salad is one of the signature dishes.
2532 Broadway (near 95th Street), Tel 212-932-00 68, 6.00–1.00, daily.

The Mermaid Inn The ultimate in New England seafood. Oysters, shrimp, mussels, lobster, and signature dishes like fresh fish with hazelnuts, garlic, and chillies are on the menu, as is the irrepressible clam chowder, which does indeed contain lots of clams.
568 Amsterdam Avenue (near 88th Street), Tel 212-799-74 00, www.themermaidnyc.com, Mon–Thurs 17.30–23.00, Fri, Sat 17.00–23.30, Sun 17.00–22.00.

Hotel Beacon is a good value for money address – for New York.

Pio Pio Another branch of the popular Peruvian restaurant best known for its rotisserie chicken. The "Matador Combo" (chicken, rice, beans, avocado salad, and fries with sausage) is the one to go for.
*702 Amsterdam Avenue
(corner 94th Street),
Tel 212-665-30 00,
www.piopionyc.com
11.00–23.00, daily.*

Rack & Soul Southern cooking Harlem-style, with fried chicken and a first-class barbecue. Sweet waffles are served with the chicken, and there's an ultra-sweet banana pudding for dessert. Plus European beers or ice tea.
*258 West 109th Street
(near Broadway),
Tel 212-222-48 00,
www.rackandsoul.com,
Mon–Thurs 11.00–22.00,
Fri 11.00–23.00, Sat 10.00–
23.00, Sun 10.00–21.30.*

West Branch A pleasant Mediterranean-style bistro with a club or sports bar atmosphere. The cheeseburgers are enormous and expensive, as are the Cuban pork sandwiches. The fish dishes are recommended.
*2178 Broadway (corner 77th Street), Tel 212-777-67 64,
Mon–Sun 17.00–23.00,
Fri, Sat 17.00–24.00,
Sun 17.00–22.00.*

ACCOMMODATION

Amsterdam Inn A good-value hotel with clean and welcoming rooms with cheerful furnishings. The cheaper rooms have no en-suite bathrooms.
*340 Amsterdam Avenue
(corner 76th Street),
Tel 212-579-75 00,
www.amsterdaminn.com*

Excelsior Hotel A good hotel on Central Park and a stone's throw from the American Museum of Natural History. The marble- and hardwood-paneled lobby boasts a European-style elegance, and the rooms also have an Old World charm.
*45 West 81st Street,
Tel 212-362-92 00,
www.excelsiorhotelny.com*

Hotel Beacon The good-value hotel was once an apartment building and a portion of the rooms are still rented out to long-stay guests. Each room has a fully fitted kitchen with a cooker and a refrigerator, and the handy Fairway supermarket is just over the road.
*2130 Broadway
(near 75th Street),
Tel 212-787-11 00,
www.beaconhotel.com*

Hotel Belleclaire A recently renovated 1903 Beaux Arts building with spacious rooms, each featuring a refrigerator

Hotel Newton offers overnight accommodation at a good price.

(very important in expensive New York), a television, and a telephone. The beds are exceptionally comfortable and the rates are good value, with a room costing a little over $100.
250 West 77th Street (corner Broadway),
Tel 212-362-77 00,
www.belleclairehotel.com

Hotel Newton Definitely one of the best of the mid-price hotels in Manhattan. For $100 you get a spacious and clean room with an en-suite bathroom. Cable TV and room service are extra, and the service is extremely friendly. The subway is just around the corner.
2528 Broadway
(near 94th Street),
Tel 212-678-65 00,
www.thehotelnewton.com

Morningside Inn This spartan mixture of hotel and guesthouse is somewhat reminiscent of a youth hostel, but the rooms are clean and very good value for money. Unfortunately the bathrooms are shared with the other residents and there is no air-conditioning.
235 West 107th Street,
Tel 212-316-00 55,
www.morningsideinn-ny.com

On the Ave Hotel Hire a penthouse here and you can enjoy the use of a private balcony with a magnificent view of Central Park, or you can save some money and use the communal balcony on the 16th floor. All the rooms feature a crisp and modern design. They're elegantly furnished and come with numerous extras; the bathrooms are fitted out in marble. It also has family rooms for 4, fitness center, restaurant, and bar.
2178 Broadway (corner 77th Street), Tel 212-362-11 00,
www.ontheave-nyc.com

36 Riverside Wyman House This bed and breakfast located right on the Riverside Park is housed in a Victorian house from 1888 and is furnished accordingly. Each of the rooms has a different theme attached – the "Amadeus" room recalls historical Vienna, while the "Angelica" is decorated with silk. Every room has a small kitchen area.
36 Riverside Drive
(corner 76th Street),
Tel 212-799-82 81,
www.wymanhouse.com

The Harlem Flophouse Tiny rooms in a renovated brownstone house belonging to the artist, Rene Calvo. This bed and breakfast establishment resembles an art gallery and antique fixtures, such as the claw-foot bathtubs, are reminiscent of Harlem's first renaissance. Owner Calvo serves the homemade breakfast personally.

The Lenox Lounge has been a great jazz venue for decades. The greats played here: Miles Davis and John Coltrane.

242 West 123rd Street (near Frederick Douglass Blvd), Tel 212-662-06 78, www.harlemflophouse.com

The Lucerne This house was built as early as 1903 as accommodation for university students, but in 1995 it underwent expensive renovations and was transformed into a comfortable and almost European boutique hotel. For the Upper West Side, this accommodation is surprisingly good value. All the rooms have wireless Internet access as well as a host of other extras.
201 West 79th Street (corner Amsterdam Avenue), Tel 212-875-10 00, www.newyorkhotel.com

The Phillips Club If you're ready and willing to shell out some $500 a day for a comfortably furnished and relatively large two-room apartment,

then this is the right place for you: there's even a microwave and a dishwasher. It's also only a few steps from the well-equipped Reebok Sports Club.
155 West 66th Street (near Broadway), Tel 212-835-88 00, www.phillipsclub.com

NIGHTLIFE

Lenox Lounge The lounge of this legendary Harlem 1940s art deco bar has been the backdrop for jazz legends, such as Billie Holiday, Miles Davis, and John Coltrane and still features reasonably good jazz. The atmospheric surroundings and the music are of a much higher standard than the rather average food.
288 Lenox Avenue (near 125th Street), Tel 202-427-02 53, www.lenoxlounge.com, 12.00–4.00, daily.

St Nick's This is how a bar must have looked in the Golden Twenties: a long counter and a tiny stage in the basement of an apartment building. It was once owned by Duke Ellington's piano player. Live jazz seven nights a week – the trad jazz is the best.
773 St. Nicolas Avenue (near W. 148th Street), Tel 212-283-97 28, www.stnicksjazzpub.net, Mon–Thurs 13.00–3.00, Fri, Sat 16.00–4.00.

Night Cafe A comfortable night café with a long bar and only a few tables. There are occasional readings and small gigs. The prize-winning owner runs a fun quiz, the winner of which is rewarded with a bottle from behind the bar.
938 Amsterdam Avenue (near 106th Street), Tel 212-864-88 89, 11.00–4.00; daily.

The Brooklyn Museum founded in Prospect Heights in 1884 shows great art on 52,000 sq m (560,000 sq ft) exhibition space.

MUSEUMS, MUSIC, DRAMA

Alice Austen House Museum
Best known for her scenes from day-to-day New York life, the photographer, (1866-1952) spent the greater part of her life in this Victorian cottage.
2 Hylan Boulevard,
Staten Island,
Tel 718-816-45 06,
www.aliceausten.org,
Mar–Dec Thurs to Sun
12.00–17.00.

American Guitar Museum
Here all music fans can admire instruments from 1840 to the present day. There is also a music store, a music school, and a luthier's workshop.
1810 New Hyde Park Road,
Tel 516-488-50 00,
www.americanguitar
museum.com,
Tues, Wed, Fri 10.00–18.00,
Thurs 10.00–22.00,
Sat 9.00–17.00.

Bronx Museum of the Arts
Founded in 1971, the Bronx museum concentrates on 20th-century and contemporary art. Special events every first Friday in the month.
1040 Grand Concourse,
Tel 718-681-60 00,
www.bronxmuseum.org,
Thurs–Sun 11.00–18.00,
Fri 11.00–20.00, .

Brooklyn Children's Museum The museum was founded in 1899. It tries to involve, challenge and inspire kids to learn about the world around them, especially technology and nature.
145 Brooklyn Avenue,
Tel 718-735-44 00,
www.brooklynkids.org,
Tues–Thurs 11.00–17.00,
Fri 11.00–19.30, Sat,
Sun 10.00–17.00.

Brooklyn Museum Founded in 1884, this is one of New York's most important collections. The exhibits are drawn from almost every genre and era of art from around the world: Ancient Egypt, the ancient world, the Near and Far East, art from Africa, Oceania, and America, of course, not to mention European and American art right up to contemporary design and photography.
200 Eastern Parkway,
Tel 718-638-50 00,
www.brooklynmuseum.org,
Wed–Fri 10.00–17.00,
Sat 11.00–18.00/23.00,
Sun 11.00–18.00.

Edgar Allan Poe Cottage A farmhouse built in 1812 and the great American writer's last residence. In 1902 it was removed from its original location near to the Poe Park and faithfully rebuilt. When Poe penned his works, he would have been able to enjoy unobstructed views of the Bronx hills.

The Ellis Island immigration museum next to the Statue of Liberty documents the story of immigration to the United States.

2640 Grand Concourse, Bronx, Tel 718-881-89 00, www.bronxhistorical society.org, Mon–Fri 9.00-17.00, Sat 10.00–16.00, Sun 13.00–17.00

Ellis Island National Monument
The museum of immigration's documentation department is housed on the site of the old immigration authority and details the history of immigration to the United States.
Ellis Island, Tel 212-363-32 06, www.nps.gov, 9.30–16.30, daily.

Fisher Landau Center for Art
Emily Fisher Landau's private collection holds prized modern art from 1960 onwards.
38–27 30th Street, Long Island City, Tel 718-937-07 27, www.flcart.org, Thurs–Mon 12.00–17.00.

Greenwood Cemetery
A romantic park dating from 1838, with over 600,000 graves, including those of Mozart's librettist Lorenzo da Ponte, Leonard Bernstein, and Lola Montez.
500 25th Street, Brooklyn, Tel 718-768-73 00, www.green-wood.com

Jacques Marchais Center of Tibetan Art
This museum resembles a Himalayan monastery and its exhibits include works of art, musical instruments, and everyday objects, providing a fascinating view of Tibetan culture.
338 Lighthouse Avenue, Staten Island, Tel 718-987-35 00, www.tibetanmuseum.org, Wed–Sun 13.00–17.00.

King Manor Museum
The country seat of Rufus King (1755–1827), an important politician who co-wrote the American constitution and fought slavery. In 1900 it was turned into a museum detailing aspects of the life and works of King and his family.
15003 Jamaica Avenue, Tel 718-206-05 45, www.kingmanor.org, Thurs–Fri 12.00–13.30, Sat, Sun 13.00–16.30 (guided tour only), closed Jan.

New York Hall of Science
Built initially as a pavilion for the 1964 World's Fair, the New York Hall of Science is now New York City's hands-on science and technology center. Since 1986, NYSCI has involved more than five million children, parents and teachers in learning about science.
47-01 111th Street, Tel 718-699-00 05, www.nyscience.org, Tues–Thurs 9.30–14.00/ 17.00 (Jul, Aug), Fri 9.30– 17.00, Sat, Sun 10.00–18.00.

The Mermaid Parade celebrates the start of the bathing season.

New York City Transit Museum

A museum dedicated to the development of public transportation in New York, with video footage and exhibits illustrating the history, construction methods, and expansion of the first New York City's subway built between 1900 and 1925. Since it's inception over a quarter century ago, the Museum, housed in a historic 1936 IND subway station in Brooklyn Heights, has grown in scope and popularity. As custodian and interpreter of the region's extensive public transportation networks, the Museum strives to share, through its public programs, this rich and vibrant history with local and international audiences.

Boerum Place/Schermerhorn Street, Brooklyn,
Tel 718-694-16 00,
www.mta.info,
Tues–Fri 10.00–16.00,
Sat, Sun 12.00–17.00.

Queens County Farm Museum

The Queens County Farm Museum dates back to 1697; it occupies New York City's largest remaining tract of undisturbed farmland, and is the only working historical farm in the city. The farm encompasses a 47-acre parcel that is the longest continuously farmed site in New York State. The site includes historic farm buildings, a greenhouse complex, livestock, farm vehicles and implements, planting fields, an orchard, and an herb garden. The mission of the Queens County Farm Museum is to preserve, restore, and interpret the site, its history and owner's lifestyles.

73–50 Little Neck Pkwy,
Floral Park, Tel 718-347-32 76,
www.queensfarm.org,
Mon–Fri 9.00–17.00
(outdoor areas),
Sat, Sun 10.00–17.00
(guided tours).

Queens Museum of Art

Housed in the New York City Building, designed for the 1939 World's Fair, the museum has a selection of contemporary art and a famous giant New York panorama built by Robert Moses for the 1964 World's Fair. From 1946 to 1950 the building was used as the headquarters of the newly formed United Nations, and then was refurbished to become the focal point of the World's Fair of 1964–65. It was last refurbished in 2005–2006.

NCY Building, Flushing
Meadows Corona Park,
Tel 718-592-97 00,
www.queensmuseum.org,
Wed–Sun 12.00–18.00,
Fri 12.00–20.00 (summer).

Sag Harbor Whaling Museum

Built in the colonial style in 1845, this country house (with a freemason's lodge on the first upper floor) houses a mu-

An ocean of pink cherry blossom forms the backdrop to the Japanese Cherry Blossom Festival.

seum charting the history of whaling and seafaring. The little port of Sag Harbor was the hub of the whaling industry in the 19th century.
200 Main Street, Sag Harbor,
Tel 631-725-07 70,
www.sagharborwhaling
museum.org,
Mon–Sat 10.00–17.00,
Sun 13.00–17.00.

Snug Harbor Cultural Center and Botanical Garden This former retirement home for seamen in the 19th-century houses a botanical garden, a theater, a concert hall, the Newhouse Center for Contemporary Art, the Staten Island Museum, and a children's museum.
1000 Richmond Terrace,
Staten Island,
Tel 718-448-25 00,
www.snug-harbor.org,
the park is open sunrise to sunset; institutions are open Tues–Sun 10.00–16.00.

Socrates Sculpture Park This was an abandoned riverside landfill until 1986 when a coalition of artists and community members transformed it into studio and exhibition space for artists and a park for local residents. Today it is an internatally renowned outdoor museum offering a wide variety of public services..
32–01 Vernon Boulevard,
Tel 718-956-18 19,
www.socratessculpture
park.org,
from 10.00 daily.

Van Cortlandt House Museum Built in 1748, this Georgian country house has been home to a museum of the 18th century since 1896. Magnificent furniture and household items.
W 246th Street/Broadway,
Tel 718-543-33 44,
www. vancortlandthouse.org,
Tues–Fri 10.00–15.00,
Sat, Sun 11.00–16.00.

FESTIVALS AND EVENTS

Cherry Blossom Festival The lovely pink blossom of the cherry trees along the Esplanade beside Brooklyn Botanic Garden is celebrated in this traditional Japanese festival, but the emphasis is just as much on Japanese culture in general, with taiko drumming, music, tea ceremonies, bonsai courses, and fashion shows.
1000 Washington Avenue,
Tel 718/623-72 00,
www.bbg.org,
first weekend in May.

DUMBO Art under the Bridge A festival organized by the artists' community DUMBO in the old port area of Brooklyn, with workshops, galleries, performances, and street art.
30 Washington Street,
Tel 718-694-08 31,
www.dumboartscenter.org,
Sept.

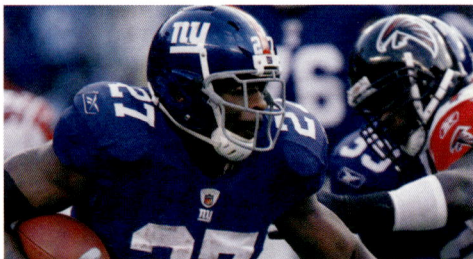

American Football ranks high in New Yorkers' interests. The New York Giants play in the National Football League.

Mermaid Parade A magnificent parade of mermaids and sea gods in all their glitz and glory proceeds along the Coney Island Boardwalk, celebrating sand, sea, and the start of summer. Afterwards there is a massive party with live music, a tombola, comedy, and burlesque shows.
Tel 718-372-51 59,
www.coneyislandusa.com,
first Sat after 21 Jun.

West Indian American Day Parade and Carnival With more than three million participants, this Caribbean-inspired festival is one of America's biggest carnivals and almost causes a state of emergency in Brooklyn. The procession lasts all day, and there are tasty Caribbean delicacies.
Eastern Parkway,
Tel 718-467-17 97,
www.wiadca.org,
first Mon in Sept.

SPORT, GAMES, FUN

American Football The Giants and the Jets are the darlings of New Yorkers. Both teams play in the NFL (National Football League), the biggest professional league of this all-American sport, and host their sold-out home games at the Giants Stadium in the Meadowlands Sports Complex in New Jersey.
East Rutherford (NJ),
Giants: Tel 201-935-82 22,
www.giants.com,
Jets. Tel 516-560-82 00,
www.newyorkjets.com,
Aug–Feb.

Baseball New York is one of the few places in the United States where baseball is held in higher regard than even American football or basketball.The regular season of both major league teams, the New York Mets (Metropolitan Baseball Club of New York) and the New York Yankees, starts in spring and runs into the Fall (after which the play-offs are held).
Mets: Tel 718-507-84 99,
http://newyork.mets.mlb.com,
Yankees: Tel 212-307-1212,
http://newyork.yankees.
mlb.com,
Apr–Oct.

Belmont Stakes New York's biggest flat race in Belmont Park in Queens is one of the three most famous horse races in the United States. The prize fund is $1 million, but admission is between $2 and $5.
Belmont Park, 2150 Hempstead Turnpike, Elmont (NY),
Tel 516-488-60 00,
www.belmontstakes.com,
Start: 9 Jun, course open: end of April–mid-Jun and Sept–Oct.

Bike New York The great 67.5-km (42-mile) "Five Boro

The Bronx Zoo was established as early as 1899.

Bike Tour" is one of the highlights of the month of May, Thousands of participants stamp on their pedals and launch themselves into an exciting race across town. Even more spectators follow – the roads are closed to traffic.
Tel 212-932-24 53,
http://bikemonthnyc.org,
May.

Bronx Zoo (Bronx Park) The largest and most interesting zoo in New York; there is also a petting zoo.
2300 Southern Boulevard,
Tel 718-220-51 00,
www.bronxzoo.com,
Mon–Fri 10.00–17.00, Sat, Sun and public hols 10.00–17.00.

Brooklyn Botanic Garden Founded in 1910 and famous for its rose garden, the Japanese gardens, and a garden for the blind, which is arranged by the scent of the flowers.
900 Washington Avenue,
Tel 718-623-72 00,
www.bbg.org,
Tues–Fri 8.00–18.00, Sat, Sun and public hols 10.00–18.00.

Coney Island, Cyclone Coney Island lost some of its appeal in more recent times. The Cyclone, however, has been one of the main attractions since 1927. A frantic trip on this rollercoaster, some of whose drops are almost vertical, has become a New York symbol and is fun for all.
1000 Surf Avenue/West 10th Street, Tel 718-372-02 75,
www.coneyislandcyclone.com,
mid-Apr–mid-Jun, Sat–Sun 12.00–18.00, mid-Jun–Sept, 12.00–24.00, daily.

Jamaica Bay Wildlife Refuge This nature reserve in Queens is also called Birdland, because there is something to see here for ornithologists and bird-watchers throughout the year. Sheltered from the Atlantic Ocean, the bay is a stopping-off point for almost 350 migratory species of birds, mostly in July and August.
Cross Bay Boulevard/Broad Channel, Tel 718-318-43 40,
www.nyharborparks.org,
www.nps.gov/gate,
open sunrise–sunset, visitor center: 8.30–17.00, daily.

National Tennis Center The U.S. Open, one of the four Grand Slam competitions, is held here at the end of August (until mid-September) and you can watch, but not play. Tickets can generally be bought as early as April (e.g. from Ticketmaster), but tickets for the big matches are usually hard to come by. After the U.S. Open is over, 33 outdoor and nine indoor courts become available; book in advance, as demand is very high.

The New York Botanical Garden boasts an area of some 100 ha (247 acres), making it one of the largest botanical gardens in the world.

Flushing Meadows Corona Park, Queens,
Tel 718-760-62 00,
www.usta.com and
www.usopen.org, Ticket-
master: Tel 212-307-71 71,
www.ticketmaster.com

New York Aquarium Large numbers of sea creatures can be seen here at the aquarium on the Boardwalk on Coney Island, from local to exotic. The feeding times of sharks, otters, and penguins are tourist magnets, as are the appearances of the beluga whales (in the winter months only) and the sea lions. The aquarium also educates on the ecosystems of the different coastal and oceanic habitats.
Surf Avenue/West Eighth Street, Tel 718-265-34 91,
www.nyaquarium.com,
10.00–17.00, daily, May–Sept:
Mon–Fri 10.00–18.00, Sat, Sun 10.00–19.00.

New York Botanical Garden (Bronx Park) One of America's largest and oldest botanical gardens, based on the Royal Botanical Gardens in London, was founded on this site on the Bronx River in 1891. Admire the orchids, palms, cacti, and tropical plants in the main building and visit the museum and herbarium in the Lorillard Snuff Mill. Other attractions include a rose garden with 2,700 different varieties and a rock garden. The Everett Children's Adventure Garden and the Ruth Rea Howell Family Garden cater for the children.
Southern Boulevard/
200th Street,
Tel 718-817-87 00,
www.nybg.org,
Tues–Sun 10.00–18.00, guided tours available.

New York City Marathon Every year, New York's famous marathon attracts tens of thousands of runners, both professional and amateur, from all over the world. It covers 42 km (26 miles 385 yards) across all five boroughs, starting on the Verrazano Narrows Bridge (Staten Island) and finishing at the Tavern on the Green in Central Park. Countless excited spectators cheer on the runners from the kerbside.
www.nycmarathon.org,
first Sun in Nov.

HEALTH AND BEAUTY

Area Emporium This spa in the middle of Cobble Hill in Brooklyn comes with a café and a store. The attached yoga studio is a block away, on Court Street (no. 320) and they also sell cosmetics and other products to improve the body and the mind.
281 Smith Street,
Tel 718-522-19 06,
www.areabrooklyn.com,

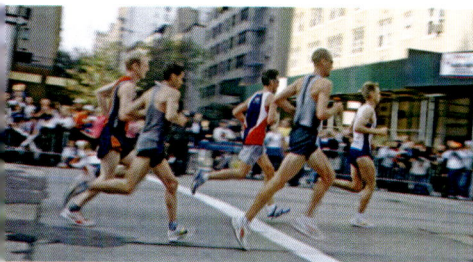

The legendary New York City Marathon starts on the first Saturday in November. Thousands of enthusiastic spectators line the roads.

10.00–19.00, daily, yoga studio: Mon–Fri 7.00–20.15, Sat–Sun 10.00–17.00.

Astoria Pool Opened in Queens in 1936, this art deco pool has a view of the Triborough Bridge. On sunny summer days, New York's oldest and largest public swimming baths can attract more than 1,000 bathers.
Astoria Park,
Tel 718-626-86 20,
Jun–Aug 11.00–19.00.

D'mai Urban Spa This spa is located in Brooklyn, but at times it feels like a resort on Bali. The interior is decorated in the style of an Indonesian healing temple and soothing natural sounds are played to induce an air of calm. You can visit the sauna, get a hand treatment, have a facial or a manicure, and much more, or just seek refuge in the cabana,

a tent offering outdoor massage for couples. Take time out to pamper yourself.
157 Fifth Avenue/Park Slope,
Tel 718-398-21 00,
www.dmaiurbanspa.com
Mon 11.00–21.00,
Tues–Fri 11.00–19.30,
Sat, Sun 10.00–19.00.

SHOPPING

Almondine Bakery Located not far from Empire Fulton Ferry State Park, this Brooklyn bakery sells fresh croissants and excellent brioche.
85 Water Street/Main Street,
Tel 718/797-50 26,
www.almondinebakery.com,
Mon–Thurs 7.00–19.00, Fri 7.00–21.00, Sat 7.00–19.00, Sun 10.00–18.00.

Burlington Coat Factory This discount fashion outlet claims to be the cheapest, and sells branded clothes, shoes, and

bags. There is a second branch on 6th Ave/W 23rd St.
625 Atlantic Avenue/
Fifth Avenue,
Tel 718-622-4057,
www.burlingtoncoat
factory.com,
Mon–Sat 10.00–21.00,
Sun 11.00–18.00.

Woodbury Commons An hour's bus ride north of New York City, this vast designer outlet mall has good deals on clothes, shoes, accessories, and much more. There are about 220 branded stores based here, such as Armani and Boss. The discounts are between 25 and 65 percent.
498 Red Apple Court, Central Valley, Tel 845-928-40 00,
www.premiumoutlets.com,
10.00–21.00, daily (except Jan–Feb: Mon–Wed 10.00–18.00, Thurs–Sun 10.00–21.00), bus timetable:
www.njtransit.com

Exploring the city of New York is exhausting, but a strong espresso is a wonderful pick-me-up.

EATING AND DRINKING

Anthony's South Italian food "just like mamma makes"; the trip is worth it for the crispy pizzas alone.
426A Seventh Avenue
(near 14th Street),
Tel 718-369-83 15,
Sun–Thurs 12.00–23.00,
Fri, Sat 12.00–24.00.

Applewood A family business in Brooklyn. The owners prefer organic produce without hormones and antibiotics – and conjures up fine dishes.
501 Eleventh Street
(near Seventh Avenue),
Tel 718-788-18 10,
www.applewoodny.com,
Tues–Fri 17.00–23.00, Sat 10.00–14.00, 17.00–23.00,
Sun 10.00–15.00.

Bacchus A French bistro with friendly staff and reasonable prices. The house specials include classics such as coq au vin and of course casseroles, pâtées, and cheeses.
409 Atlantic Avenue
(near Bond Street),
Tel 718-852-15 72,
www.bacchusbistro.com,
Mon–Fri 17.00–23.00,
Sat, Sun 10.30–24.00.

Bamonte's Banks of chandeliers illuminate the antique-filled dining room of this Italian restaurant, one of Brooklyn's most popular since the 1950s, and the food, such as classic antipasti, cheese ravioli, and lasagne with cheese and spinach, definitely won't be a disappointment.
32 Withers Street,
Tel 718-384-88 31,
Mon, Wed, Thurs 12.00–22.30, Fri 12.00–23.00, Sat 13.00–23.00, Sun 13.00–22.00
.

Bittersweet This tiny bar opposite Fort Greene Park in Brooklyn has strong espresso and delicate ice cream in variations such as "Jamaican grape nut" (vanilla with cornflakes). As a contrast to these sugary treats, they also have tasty vegetarian sandwiches on the menu.
180 Dekalb Avenue
(near Carlton Avenue),
Tel 718-852-25 56,
Mon–Fri 7.00–19.00,
Sat, Sun 7.30–19.00.

Blackbird Parlour A friendly, European-style coffee house. The Italian espresso is strong and tasty, and the cappuccino and café latte much classier than the competition There are also cookies, delivered fresh daily from the famous Artopolis bakery in Astoria.
197 Bedford Avenue (corner North Sixth Street),
Tel 718-599-27 07,
Mon–Fri 8.00–22.00,
Sat, Sun 10.00–3.00.

Porterhouse steaks are the specialty at the Peter Luger Steak House, they come pre-cut on a hot plate and continue cooking at your table.

Bogota Latin Bistro The walls are resplendent with bright murals of South American themes, and the favourite Central South American food is served up here. All the dishes, but especially the steaks and the chicken, are spicy and hot.
141 Fifth Avenue (near St. John's Place),
Tel 718-230-38 05,
www.bogotabistro.com,
Mon, Wed, Thurs 17.00–23.00, Fri, Sat 17.00–1.00,
Sun 12.00–22.00.

Café Glechik Brighton Beach is inhabited by Russian immigrants who have spotted a good thing in this Ukrainian café. There are plentiful soups and stews, such as green borscht with eggs and rice. The cabbage roulade is one of their most delicious main courses.
3159 Coney Island Avenue (Avenue),
Tel 718-616-04 94,
10.00–22.00, daily.

Choice Market This is a rather special health food: you won't find just shoots and seeds here, but instead creative and tasty dishes such as grilled tuna with a spicy Amarillo sauce and olive oil.
318 Lafayette Avenue (corner Grand Avenue),
Tel 718-230-52 34,
6.00–21.00, daily.

Faan A modern Asiatic restaurant with outstanding noodle dishes from Japan, China, Thailand, and Vietnam.
209 Smith Street (corner Baltic Street),
Tel 718-694-22 77,
11.00–23.00, daily.

Fette Sau A BBQ restaurant in an old car workshop. Known as "Fat Sow" in German, you'll find Italian sausage and chicken, and barbecued lamb.
354 Metropolitan Avenue,
Tel 714-963-34 04,
Sun–Thurs 17.00–2.00,
Fri, Sat 17.00–4.00.

Five Front A friendly and atmospheric bistro beneath Brooklyn Bridge. This little bar is famed for its excellent mussels, but also serves fast food, such as chicken fingers and spare ribs. Good wine list.
5 Front Street (near Old Fulton Street),
Tel 718-625-55 59,
www.fivefrontrestaurant.com,
Mon, Wed, Thurs 17.30–23.00, Fri 17.30–24.00,
Sat 11.00–24.00.

Peter Luger Steak House The best steakhouse in New York, listed at the top in the respected Zagat guide for the last 30 years. It serves only porterhouse steaks for two, three, or even four people.

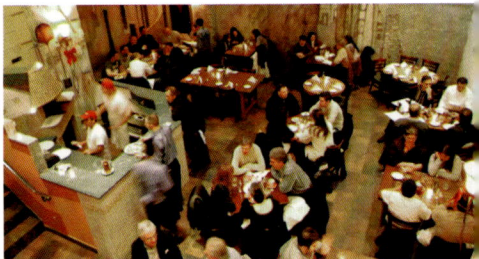

Zero Otto Nove is a cheerful trattoria opened in 1884. Try one of the first-class pizzas from the wood oven.

The family select the meat themselves.
178 Broadway (in Brooklyn), www.peterluger.com, Tel 718-387-74 00, Mon–Thurs 11.45–21.45, Fri, Sat 11.45–22.45, Sun 12.45–21.45.

South Fin Grill In addition to the magnificent view of the Verrazzano Bridge, the fish dishes have Mediterranean spices and taste fantastic; you'll even find sushi rolls with cooked eel and peach on the menu.
300 Father Capodanno Boulevard (corner Sand Lane), Tel 718-447-76 79, Sept–May: Tues–Thurs 11.00–21.30, Fri, Sat 11.00–23.00, Sun 11.00–21.00; Jun–Aug: also Mon 11.00–21.30.

Uncle Peter's Bar and Grill Uncle Peter is an Italian called Ernesto who has spent time in Argentina, and he unites the cooking of the two countries in an interesting and tasty fusion. Steaks and ravioli appear on the same plate; later you will be entertained with Argentine-an tango music.
83–15 Northern Boulevard (near 83rd Street), Tel 718-615-86 00, Mon–Fri 12.00–22.00, Sat 16.00–23.00, Sun 13.00–22.00.

Wave Thai Thai cooking in an elegant lounge atmosphere. Fresh fish is spiced up in the wok into a variety of curries.
21–37 31st Street (near Ditmars Road), Tel 718-777-67 89, www.wavethainyc.com, Mon–Thurs 11.00–23.00, Fri 11.00–24.00, Sat 12.00–24.00, Sun 12.00–23.00.

Zero Otto Nove You can eat well in the Bronx, especially in this atmospheric trattoria, where the pizzas come out of the wood oven topped with the freshest ingredients.
2357 Arthur Avenue (near 186th Street), Tel 718-220-10 27, www.roberto089.com, Tues–Thurs 12.00–14.30, 16.30–22.00, Fri, Sat 12.00–14.30, 16.30–23.00, Sun 13.00–21.00.

ACCOMMODATION

Baisley House The interior decorator has installed a friendly bed and breakfast in this romantic brownstone building, owned by a merchant, Charles Baisley in the 19th century. The Victorian décor is reminiscent of America at the time of the Founding Fathers.
294 Hoyt Street (near Sacket Street), Tel 718-935-19 59

Dekoven Suites This is actually more of a sub-let. The owner has fitted out the cella

The Sofia Inn is a comfortable b&b, which also boasts its own small garden behind the house.

of her Victorian house in Brooklyn as a luxury flat with a kitchen and bathroom
*30 Dekoven Court
(near Rugby Road),
Tel 718-421-10 52,
www.bbonline.de*

Golden Gate Inn If Manhattan is too expensive, you may find this simple but clean hotel just right. The rooms cost less than $100, although you have to take the nearby highway and the less-than-attractive surroundings into account.
*3867 Shore Parkway
(near Bragg Street),
Tel 718-743-40 00,
www.goldengateinnny.com*

Sheraton LaGuardia East Hotel Not a typical airport hotel. Although only 5 km (3 miles) away from LaGuardia Airport in Queens, the hotel is best known for its large collection of Asiatic antiques;

even the décor is Asian-influenced. The beds are comfortable and the service is exemplary.
*135–20 39th Avenue
(near Main Street),
Tel 718-460-66 66,
www.starwoodhotels.com*

The Sofia Inn bed and breakfast is situated in a brownstone building in the heart of Brooklyn. You can choose from a three-room suite with a sitting room, kitchen, and bathroom, or four smaller rooms with bathrooms in the hall.
*288 Park Place (near Vanderbilt Avenue),
Tel 718-398-41 85,
www.brooklynbedand
breakfast.net*

The New York Marriott at Brooklyn Bridge Situated just across the river from Manhattan, this hotel offers more than just magnificent views that can be enjoyed from most rooms.

The hotel also offers extras like Internet access, newspapers, and free coffee.
*333 Adams Street (near Willoughby Street),
Tel 718-246-70 00,
www.brooklynmarriott.com*

NIGHTLIFE

Remote Sports Bar An atmospheric sports bar in Queens – televisions on the wall have live transmissions of matches.
*2701 23rd Avenue
Tel 718-728-22 58,
Mon–Fri 11.00–2.00,
Sat, Sun 10.00–2.00.*

The Diamond A bar selling an extensive selection of low-alcohol beer.
*43 Franklin Street
(near Calyer Street),
Tel 718-383-50 30,
www.thediamondbrooklyn.com,
Sun–Wed 17.00–1.00,
Thurs–Sat 17.00–2.00.*

The Rose Center for Earth and Space has been an attraction at the American Museum of Natural History since February 2000. An impressive earth globe of 27 m (89 ft) diameter floats in a glass and steel cube.

New York is is a city bursting with extraordinary architecture and stunning museums with unrivaled 20th-century art collections such as the Museum of Modern Art, the Solomon R. Guggenheim Foundation, and the Whitney Museum of American Art, to name but some of the larger ones. Lovers of pre-20th-century art can find treasures too, particularly at the Metropolitan Museum and the Frick Collection, which boast works by the most famous artists in the western world. The museums of natural history, ethnology, and those showing the history and culture of the American continent should not be missed.

MAJOR MUSEUMS

The setting for the film *Night at the Museum*, the Natural History Museum has one of the greatest natural history collections in the world; with over 30 million specimens it is also the largest in the world. But the museum does not just cover the continent of America. Its remit is the study and evolution of all living things on the planet. Its highly impressive and comprehensive collections deserves at least one day to be set aside for your visit. Designed by Calvert Vaux and Jacob Wrey Mould, the museum complex was built between 1877 and 1935 and is entered through John Russell Pope's monumental Theodore Roosevelt Memorial Wing, guarded by James Fraser's 1940 equestrian statue of the president. The latest addition is James Stewart Polshek's Rose Center for Earth and Space which was built in 2000. Also located in this new complex is the Hayden Planetarium.

THE MUSEUM

This museum of natural science and ethnology was founded as early as 1869, and is thus the oldest in the city. Comprising 20 buildings, some of which are five floors high, spread over four blocks, this giant museum has something for every adult and child – one day is simply not enough to see everything! The permanent display is complemented with long-running special exhibitions, and an internationally recognized research department with its own laboratories assists the museum's curators.

THE COLLECTIONS

The Museum of Natural History is principally famous for its habitat dioramas illustrating the development of life on our planet – preserved animals are shown in their natural environment – and for its numerous departments which use the most up-to-date scientific techniques to research the development of life and civilization on earth. It is also known for its conservation work. The collection's most important sections, whose informative displays are often shown across several exhibition halls, are listed below.

FOSSILS

The giant skeletons and models on display in the dinosaur hall are a particular draw for young and old alike, and the museum's spectacular fossil collection is the largest in the world, offering an impressive overview of the development of vertebrates. Direct evolutionary connections and relationships between individual species are presented using the latest technology.

MAMMALS

You can increase your knowledge of the animal kingdom by studying the appearance, behavior, and native habitat of a variety of living and sometimes extinct mammals from around the globe. The focus of the collection is on animals from the continents of Asia, Africa, and North America.

BIRDS

The museum boasts a comprehensive collection of specimens from New York and North America, as well as a variety of bird species from around the world.

ANTHROPOLOGY DEPARTMENT

The museum's research work in the field of anthropology has involved numerous famous

AMERICAN MUSEUM OF NATURAL HISTORY

Left: The vast museum complex extends across four entire blocks. Architecturally it features a mixture of styles up to the present day.
Below: Fascinating prehistory – the skeleton of an Allosaurus.
Bottom: the display on biodiversity gives food for thought.

MAJOR MUSEUMS

THE DZANGA-SANGHA-RAINFOREST

This diorama of a tropical rainforest in the south-west corner of the Central African Republic gives visitors an impression of the natural beauty and enormous variety of the local plants and animals – from insects to reptiles, birds, small mammals, lowland gorillas, to forest elephants – in their natural environment. In reality, the actual area of rainforest shown here was highly endangered by large-scale forest-clearing and mining rights concessions which had been granted to foreign companies, and its chances of survival were slim. In an exemplary case of successful conservation of

scientists, including Margaret Mead and Franz Boas, and offers an insight into the cultures of Africa, North, Middle, and South America, and the Pacific Basin. Special reference is made to various Native American tribes because the museum's principal focus is on the anthropology of the American continent.

HALL OF BIODIVERSITY

More than 30 m (100 feet) long, the "Spectrum of Life" installation illustrates the evolution of microorganisms into mammals.

A stroll through the life-size Dzanga-Sangha Rainforest, complete with sounds and scents, is intended to give visitors an idea both of its biodiversity and of the dangers facing this delicate ecosystem. Human intervention and the destruction of natural habitats

are also explored, as are the ecological crisis we now face and the various approaches to conservation.

OTHER HALLS

There are also separate halls dedicated to reptiles and primates; the "Ocean Life Hall" has a life-size replica of a blue whale. Man's evolution is dealt with in a further hall, and the Arthur Ross Hall of Meteorites boasts Ahnighito, a piece of one of the largest meteorites ever to strike the earth, which was discovered in 1897 and weighs 34 tons (3,400kg).

The Hall of Minerals and Gems features such jewels as the famous "Star of India" – at 563 carats, the world's largest cut diamond; a 100-carat ruby; and the "Brazilian Princess", a 21,237-carat topaz thought to be the world's largest cut gemstone.

ROSE CENTER OF EARTH AND SPACE

Affiliated to the museum, this research and exhibition complex houses the Hayden Planetarium and exhibitions dealing with astronomy and space. The museum's IMAX cinema shows nature films and multimedia presentations on a giant screen, including the new show *Journey to the Stars* which travels through space and time to experience the life and death of the stars in the night sky, including our own nurturing sun.

American Museum of Natural History, Central Park West/79th St, Tel 212-769-5100,
www.amnh.org,
10.00–17.45, daily, Fri to 20.45,
Subway 79th St, 81st St.

Right: the model of a blue whale in the Hall of Ocean Life.

diversity and a natural way of life, the Central African Republican government initiative saw the area declared the Dzang-Ndoki National Park, a fully protected conservation district completely given over to the indigenous people for their own use covering 457,900 ha (over 1 million acres). Thus it was eventually possible to create a signpost for the conservation of natural living conditions and the enormous biodiversity in Africa that would be encouraging for the entire continent.

Left: a beautiful yellow flower in the rainforest diorama.

MAJOR MUSEUMS

The Solomon R. Guggenheim Foundation owns one of the world's greatest collections of modern art, with branches in Las Vegas/United States (the Guggenheim Hermitage), Venice/Italy (the Peggy Guggenheim Collection), Bilbao/Spain (Museo Guggenheim), Berlin/Germany (Deutsche Guggenheim), and Abu Dhabi/UAE which all complement its base in Manhattan. There was also a branch in the New York district of SoHo in 1992 to 2002.

Looking more like a sculpture than a building, the world-renowned inverted spiral of this distinctive building is the work of Frank Lloyd Wright (1867–1959), the greatest American architect of the 20th century. The building has become an icon of modern architecture. It is the perfect stage for the presentation of this comprehensive collection of high-carat works representing the best in the world of modern art works.

THE FOUNDER, SOLOMON R. GUGGENHEIM

An industrialist, mine-owner, and copper magnate from a German-Swiss family of Jewish émigrés, Solomon Robert Guggenheim (1861–1949) was the son of Meyer Guggenheim, a co-owner of the firm Guggenheim Brothers, one of America's richest men and a passionate art collector. Initially he collected Old Masters, but these were auctioned off by his heirs in 1961. However, influenced by Baroness Hilla Rebay von Ehrenwiesen, a German painter, Guggenheim turned his attention to the modernist movement, which was gaining momentum in Europe in the late 1920s, and he went on to support numerous avant-garde artists through the generous purchase of their works. He thus laid the foundations for the gigantic art empire that was to become the Solomon R. Guggenheim Foundation, endowed in 1937. The collection was made accessible to the public for the first time in a museum opened in 1939, and in 1943 Guggenheim commissioned architect Frank Lloyd Wright to design a new, dedicated exhibition museum building in the heart of New York.

THE MUSEUM BUILDING ITSELF

Wright's building, a 20th-century architectural icon, was first planned in 1943. However, construction did not begin until 1956, due to the death of Guggenheim and the financial and planning difficulties that had first to be overcome. The architect himself died six months before the museum's completion in 1959.

Wright's individual approach and spare formal architectural vocabulary, dispensing with ornamentation, made him one of the greatest architects of the 20th century. Today the distinctive, helical museum building is considered the masterpiece of his later work. It has attracted much – and ongoing – criticism since its creation: principally that the architecture detracted from the works of art and that the hanging conditions for the paintings were not the best. Whatever your own reaction to the building, it certainly exercises a great fascination on any visitor. On reaching the top by elevator, visitors walk down a curved ramp beneath a glass dome, admiring the artwork displayed on the walls and in little alcoves. In 1992, the museum was extended with a building designed by the architectural office of Charles Gwathmey and Robert Siegel. This has provided more room for the

SOLOMON R. GUGGENHEIM MUSEUM

Left: Located opposite Central Park in Fifth Avenue, the museum building itself is a work of art too.
Below: Visitors work their way down a helix-shaped ramp, admiring the works of art they pass on each floor.

MAJOR MUSEUMS

AND WHY SHOULDN'T THERE BE YELLOW COWS?

A typical work by Franz Marc, a member of the Munich "Blue Rider" group of artists, showing a leaping yellow cow with blue spots on its hide (1911). For Marc, the cheerful yellow represented femininity and gentleness, and yet the orange-red tones of the landscape render it rather unreal. Marc often retai-ned recognizable objects in his pictures, with a particular predilection for animals, whose essence he considered innocent and natural, and yet "natural" animals and landscapes were compromised as two-dimensional forms with unnatural hues. Franz Marc thus succeeded in drawing the attention of the

permanent exhibition, an auditorium, as well as sufficient place to houses the administrative offices.

THE COLLECTION

The focus of the original collection were early modernist paintings, with important works by Wassily Kandinsky, Piet Mondrian, Fernand Léger, and Robert Delaunay, among others. In 1948 the museum's holdings were augmented with a bequest from the Cologne art dealer Karl Nierendorf, who had emigrated to New York. This included works by Paul Klee, Lyonel Feininger, Joan Miró, and Marc Chagall, as well as further pieces by Kandinsky. These extended the collection with important expressionist and surrealist works. In 1963 the museum acquired the Justin K. Thannhauser Collection, which was once the property of the Munich gallery owner Heinrich Thannhauser and his son, so enriching the collection with impressionist and Post-Impressionist works, as well as some early modernist pieces and several remarkable Picassos.

There were also some small sculptures by Edgar Degas and Aristide Maillol. The museum now owns one of the world's largest public collections of Picasso's works, including *Woman with Yellow Hair* (1931) and *Le Moulin de la Galette* (1900). Acquisition of the Count Panza di Biumo's Collection brought the museum more modern works by American artists of the 1960s and 1970s, minimalist pieces, conceptual artworks, and environments by Donald Judd and Dan Flavin, among others. The Robert Mapplethorpe Foundation and the Bohen Foundation donated photos, films, and video installations. Katherine S. Dreier also bequeathed important sculptures by Constantin Brancusi, Alexander Archipenko, and Alexander Calder, to mention just some of the most important acquisitions and bequests to the Guggenheim Museum in the years since the founder's death.

Along with the artists mentioned above, the Guggenheim Museum has works by Edouard Manet, Vincent van Gogh, Paul Cézanne, Amedeo Modigliani, Georges Braque, Oscar Kokoschka, Kurt Schwitters, Alberto Giacometti, Jackson Pollock, Mark Rothko, and Robert Rauschenberg, as well as Andy Warhol, Claes Oldenburg, Walter De Maria, John Baldessari, Joseph Beuys, Mario Merz, and Rebecca Horn. The museum therefore provides an incomparable overview of art from the middle of the 19th century to the present day. The

GUGGENHEIM MUSEUM

observer away from mere recognition of externalities toward a more profound form of engagement with nature, essence, and the spiritual aspects of a motif. He used color as a means to convey spiritual elements.

Left: Franz Marc's *The Yellow Cow* (1911).

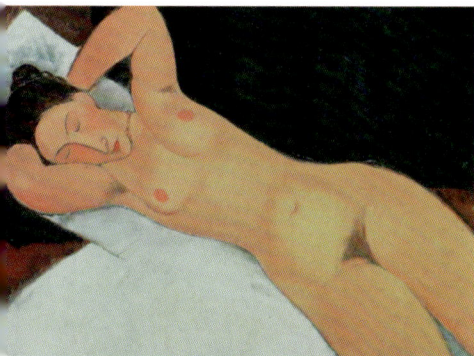

museum's comprehensive holdings allow several special exhibitions a year to run concurrently with the permanent exhibition .A recent special exhibition highlighted the history of the museum itself and of its collection, "The Guggenheim: The Making of a Museum". Thanks to a successful three-year plan of restoration, the Frank Lloyd Wright–designed building is today even more breathtaking than ever.

Guggenheim Museum,
1071 Fifth Avenue,
Tel 212-423-35 00,
www.guggenheim.org,
Mon–Wed, Fri 10.00–17.45,
Sat 10.00–19.45,
Subway 86th St.

Left top: Amedeo Modigliani's *Nude with Necklace* (1917).
Beow: Paul Cézanne's *Still Life: Flask, Glass, and Jug* (c. 1877)

MAJOR MUSEUMS

With 20 curatorial departments that are probably unique in the world, this renowned museum offers a journey through the entire history of art and culture from the Stone Age to the present day, all presented in lavish detail. The complex also houses the largest art library in the United States, a provenance research department because the museum is regularly accused of possessing stolen art, and the Cloisters annex, which showcases medieval art in a unique historical setting in the north of Manhattan. This museum of superlatives is housed in a vast complex of buildings by Central Parl, constructed between 1879 and 1913, which has been extended several times since. Although it boasts an impressive exhibition space comprising more than 300 galleries and halls, it is far too small for its collection of 3.3 million art objects so that only a fraction of the holdings can ever be exhibited at any one time.

THE HISTORY OF THE MUSEUM

In 1869, a circle of wealthy New Yorkers led by John Jay founded an art collection for the education of the city's citizens. Three years later it was recognized as an official public museum, and in 1881 was able to move into its own premises on Central Park. Countless acquisitions and donations, some of which remained separate entities, such as the Robert Lehman Collection, soon allowed the museum to grow to an impressive size. The areas covered by the collections include Islamic, ancient Middle Eastern, Pacific, African, and pre-Columbian American art, and the Far East, as well as medieval and 20th-century European art. The museum also exhibits weapons and armor, drawings, prints, photographs, and musical instruments.

EGYPTIAN ART

The exhibits range from the Old Kingdom in Egypt to the Christian era, including tombs such as the Mastaba Tomb of Perneb, the statues of Demedji and Hennutsen from 2450 BC, as well as statues of Hatshepsut, gold jewelry, glass art, and the Temple of Dendur.

GREEK AND ROMAN ANTIQUITIES

Starting with the Cycladic idols (c. 5000 to 1600 BC), this department has ancient statues, grave stele, the *Calyx-krater with Theatrical Scene* (c. 400–390 BC), and the famous *Girl with Doves* grave stele (c. 440 BC) from the Classical period, as well as Roman copies of Greek masterpieces such as Praxiteles' *Aphrodite*, the so-called "Badminton sarcophagus" (a marble sarcophagus with the Triumph of Dionysos and the Seasons), Roman wall art, an Etruscan triumphal chariot, and much more.

EUROPEAN SCULPTURE AND ART

One of the museum's highlights is the collection of European painting, sculpture, and handicrafts. Almost all the great names from the 13th to the 19th centuries are represented, including works by Giotto, Duccio, Jan van Eyck, Botticelli, Raphael, Bellini, Dürer, Titian, Bronzino, Brueghel, El Greco, Caravaggio, Rubens, Rembrandt, Frans Hals, Vermeer, Ruysdael, Poussin, Georges de La Tour, Velazquez, Chardin, Boucher, David, Goya, Turner, Manet, Vincent van Gogh, 37 canvases by Monet, 21 by Cézanne, and about 100 works by Degas – to name but a few. There are

METROPOLITAN MUSEUM OF ART

Left: The Metropolitan Museum of Art is the largest museum in the western hemisphere.
Below: statue of Sahure, a pharaoh of the Fifth Dynasty of the Old Kingdom in Egypt.

also small-scale Renaissance sculptures and whole room interiors from various periods, from Europe, to illustrate trends in western art.

AMERICAN ART(S) AND CRAFTS

The art and culture of modern America, as instanced by authentically decorated rooms, architectural features, and original utensils from the 17th to the 19th centuries, including pieces by Tiffany, and paintings and sculptures by American artists like Copley, West, Cole, a member of the Hudson River School, Hicks, Whistler, Singer Sargent, Cassatt, and Homer.

20TH-CENTURY PAINTING

American realism is represented by Edward Hopper's work, for example, and American

MAJOR MUSEUMS

CONTEMPLATING WISDOM

Thirty exhibition rooms are dedicated to European paintings of five centuries. One of the most extraordinary and outstanding works in this exhibition is Rembrandt's *Aristotle Contemplating a Bust of Homer*. Painted in 1653 for the Sicilian nobleman Don Antonio Ruffo, this picture by Rembrandt (1606–1669) shows the great ancient Greek philosopher Aristotle (384–322 BC) as a successful older man. His clothes are anything but historically correct: he wears a broad, black hat and a white coat with wide sleeves plus a dark overcoat. He wears a golden chain with a likeness of

abstract impressionism, including works by Jackson Pollock, Mark Rothko, Willem de Kooning,and Barnett Newman. There are also pieces by European artists, including Joan Miró, Pablo Picasso, Max Beckmann, Paul Klee, Amedeo Modigliani, and Henri Matisse.

EAST ASIA

The artworks in this department date from the second millennium BC to the early 20th century; of special interest are the reconstruction of a garden courtyard from ancient China, the Astor Court, Chinese Ming furniture, Buddhist sculpture, Japanese lacquerwork, jade objects, and Korean and Indian art.

FABRICS AND FASHION

A collection of more than 45,000 specimens of textiles allows the visitor to gain an overview of changing fashions from the last seven centuries. Male and female styles, children's clothes, traditional folklore clothing, modern haute couture, and current accessories are displayed. Highlights include doublets from the 17th century, Chanel pieces from the 20th century through to 21st-century designs from icons such as Vivienne Westwood. Fashion students and should head to this collection for inspiration and education.

THE CLOISTERS

This branch of the museum located in Fort Tryon Park in northern Manhattan is of even greater importance than the medieval department in the main building. The complex, acquired through a donation by John D. Rockefeller Jr to house the George Grey Bernard collection of medieval art and objects from his own collection, was assembled from fragments of European monasteries, with a few modern additions. Romanesque and Gothic sculptures, frescoes, stained-glass windows, the famous *Hunt of the Unicorn* tapestries, a book of hours that belonged to the Duc de Berry, carvings from Tilman Riemenschneider, and RobertCampin's *Mérode Triptych* are all highlights of the exhibition.

Metropolitan Museum of Art, 1000 Fifth Avenue/82nd St, Tel 212-535-77 10, www.metmuseum.org, Tues–Thurs, Sun 9.30–17.30, Fri, Sat 9.30–21.00, Subway 86th St.

Right top: Édouard Manet's *Boating* (1874), oil on canvas.
Below: Winslow Homer's *Snap the Whip I* (1872), oil on canvas

the conqueror, Alexander the Great, the most famous of Aristotle's pupils, draped around his body. Athough all the insignia indicate his superficial dignity the wise man appears full of doubt: Aristotle's right hand is contemplatively laid on the bust of the old, blind epic poet and myth maker, Homer. Transcending all worldliness and externalities, this gesture reveals contemplation – and thus his real, inner greatness.

Rembrandt Harmenszoon van Rijn's *Aristotle Contemplating a Bust of Homer* **(1653), oil on canvas.**

MAJOR MUSEUMS

The Museum of Modern Art, or MoMA for short, boasts the world's greatest collection of modern and contemporary art. Located in Midtown, the museum has paintings, sculpture, graphic design, book illustration, architectural plans, film, photography, electronic media, and design, including many design classics in its collection. The spectacular special exhibitions have only increased the museum's international fame, making it almost a pilgrimage destination for modern art aficionados.

The main building, which the MoMA moved into in 1939, is in the International Style, a term used in a 1932 exhibition at MoMA to describe the new formal vocabulary of architecture. Philip Johnson provided side extensions and the sculpture garden in 1951 and 1964, and Cesar Pelli added the tower in 1982. The museum continues to grow: a new extension was added and the

A FASCINATING IDEA IS BORN

New York 1929: Abby Aldrich Rockefeller, Lillie P. Bliss, and Mary Quinn Sullivan, three very wealthy society ladies, open a museum. And they took on the task not only of collecting and curating exclusively modern art, but also of disseminating modern trends in art and bringing them to public attention. Extensive, spectacular exhibitions held in the MoMA, as the new museum was soon called, was what the three millionaire ladies had in mind, and they were to become the focus in establishing avant-garde movements in architecture, design, and art. The institution still regards the promotion of the understanding of modern art as one of its principal tasks. After initial temporary accommodation in an office building and the Rockefeller's townhouse, the museum moved in 1939 to its own premises, designed by the architects Philip Goodwin and Edward Durell Stone. The most recent extension and renovation was conducted by the Japanese architect, Yoshio Taniguchi. The façade of the building is clear, smooth, and consists of glass and marble. The name MoMA is clearly visible from afar, in large letters.

THE FOCUS OF THE COLLECTION

Complemented by its famous special exhibitions, the museum's permanent collection gives a comprehensive overview of developments in art since 1880. Important Impressionist works are represented, as well as works from artists anticipating fauvism, expressionism, and modernism, including Vincent van Gogh's *Starry Night* from 1889, Monet's *Waterlilies* from around 1920 and works by Georges Seurat, Toulouse-Lautrec, Degas, Gauguin, Cézanne, the scurrilous James Ensor, and Modigliani. MoMA also has the world's largest collection of works by Matisse. Paintings from the early 20th century on view include *Red Studio*, *Music*, *Dance* and *Blue Window*.

There are a number of German expressionist pieces by Ernst Ludwig Kirchner and examples of cubism, whose beginnings are perhaps suggested by Picasso's 1907 canvas, *Les Demoiselles d'Avignon*, and whose highpoint is represented by further masterpieces by Picasso, Georges Braque, and Juan Gris. Visitors to MoMA are also confronted with the first movements toward abstraction, Dadaism, and surrealism in works by Paul Klee, Kurt Schwitters, Joan Miró, Max Ernst, René

MUSEUM OF MODERN ART

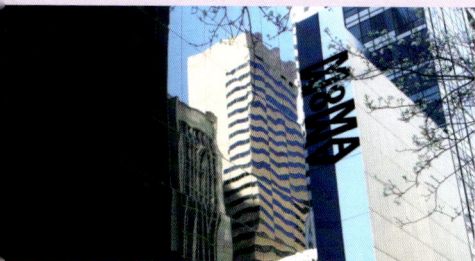

museum renovated between 2002 and 2004.

Left: The MoMA, one of the world's greatest art museums, attracts nearly two millon visitors each year with its collection and its special exhibitions.
Below: Paul Cezanne, *L'Estaque* (1882/83).

MAJOR MUSEUMS

LIGHT ON CANVAS

Impressionism perhaps represented the first attempts at modernist painting. The artists if this style were concerned with nothing less than the formal dissolution of the recognizable subject in color and light. Two-dimensional representation instead of a depth of field, the omission of the horizon– a kind of immersion of the observer in the picture – a new way of looking was postulated. Impressionism was typified by sketchy, stippled brush strokes, and Claude Monet (1840– 1926), born in Paris, is the prime exponent of the style. Although he remained wedded to representational

Magritte, and Salvador Dalí. The first half of the 20th century is rounded off with a collection of Italian futurist works ,Giorgiode Chirico's pittura metafisica, Russian constructivism, and works by American realists complete the picture of the first half of the 20th century.

Post-World War II abstract impressionism is represented with action paintings by Jackson Pollock, color field paintings by Mark Rothko and Barnett Newman, as well as Willem de Kooning's aggressive brushwork. The drift of the 20th-century art scene from Europe, most especially Paris, toward New York is also depicted: pop art, minimalism, and conceptual art constituted the next big breakthrough and these are represented with works by Robert Rauschenberg, Andy Warhol, Jasper Johns, Jim Dine, Roy Lichten-

stein, and Claes Oldenburg. The best-represented American minimalist and conceptual artists are Donald Judd and Dan Flavin. The MoMA has found room for installations, video art, and trends from the last few decades, including works by Joseph Beuys, Chuck Close, Cy Twombly, and Gerhard Richter, among others

THE ABBY ALDRICH ROCKEFELLER SCULPTURE GARDEN

The Abby Aldrich Rockefeller Sculpture Garden is one of the undisputed highlights of the museum, displaying a collection of classical modernist masterpieces from such internationally renowned sculptors as Auguste Rodin, Aristide Maillol, Jacques Lipchitz, Joan Miró, Alexander Calder, and Henry Moore. Pablo Picasso's sculpture, *She Goat* (1950) and Alberto

Giacometti's *Tall Figure 111* *(1960)* are amongst the celebrated works on show. There are also great examples of pop art and minimalist pieces by Claes Oldenburg, Ellsworth Kelly, and Donald Judd.

FILM AND PHOTOGRAPHY

The museum's international film collection is the largest in the United States and includes early works such as Louis Lumière's *Sortie d'usine* from 1895 and Edwin S. Porter's *The Life of an American Fireman* from 1903. The photographic collection dates back further, to the beginning of the medium, around 1839, and also includes work by leading contemporary artists from the most recent past. There are stills old and new here for visitors to see, and moving pictures can be watched in the video gallery. The basis for the

painting, he made a radical break from academic painting. Most Impressionists – such as Auguste Renoir, Edgar Degas, Édouard Manet, and Camille Pissarro – worked in France.

Left: Claude Monet, *Reflections of Clouds on the Water-Lily Pond* (1920).

collection was first established by the renowned Luxembourg-born photographer Edward Steichen (1879–1973),who organized the famous Family of Man photographic exhibition here in 1955 and became the collection's first curator. Subsequently, this exhibition was a major contributing factor in the recognition of photography as an independent art form in its own right.

*Museum of Modern Art,
11 West 53rd St,
Tel 212-708-94 00,
www.moma.org,
Wed–Mon 10.30–17.30,
Fri to 20.00,
Subway 49th St, Fifth
Avenue, Rockefeller Center.*

Left top: Vincent van Gogh, *Starry Night* (1889).
Below: Henri de Toulouse-Lautrec, *Miss Eglantine's Troupe* (1896).

A stroll around Greenwich Village wil take you through busy streets but also into quiet, hostorical, residential parts.

CITY WALKS

Architectural milestones, world-class museums and art galleries, imposing cathedrals, temples of big business, stores to satisfy the most demanding shoppers, plus fascinating street life – New York has it all. The city is overwhelming, and so is the sheer number of remarkable things to do and see. But if you choose your routes carefully, you can explore many sights and scenes on just a few walks. And if you do get tired, why not stop in Central Park or Prospect Park in Brooklyn for a relaxing break amidst the city's green spaces? Then take a culinary trip around the wonderful restaurants and bars that make New York a gourmet's paradise.

St Paul's Chapel is the oldest church in Manhattan.

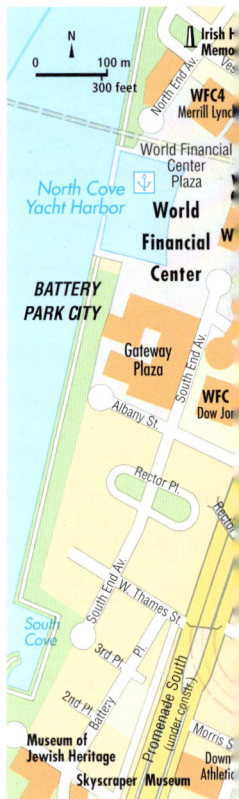

SIGHTS

❶ Tweed Courthouse New York's oldest county courthouse is located behind the City Hall on Chambers Street. A charming neo-classical building with an ornate design, it was named after William M. Tweed (1823–1828), who unfortunately is now generally known for corruption.

❷ Park Row This legendary street is in the Financial District. Its nickname, "Newspaper Row", can be traced back to the vicious circulation battle fought by several newspapers based here in the 19th century; it was originally called Chatham Street. The *New York World*, the *New York Tribune*, and the *New York Times* are just some of the 15 papers that were printed here due to the street's proximity to City Hall in the Financial District.

❸ City Hall This is the oldest council building in the United States still to house a municipal administration. It was built between 1803 and 1812 by Joseph F. Mangin and John McComb in a French neo-classical style and has an Alabama sandstone façade. In the 19th century, the state governor, whose official residence was in Albany, stayed in the Governor's Room on the first floor in City Hall during his visits to New York.

❹ Woolworth Building The Woolworth Building, built between 1910 and 1913 to a height of 241 m (790 ft), was celebrated upon its completion as the eighth wonder of the world. Franklin Winfield Woolworth paid the $13.5 million costs for the construction in cash and the design was undertaken by Cass Gilbert, the renowned architect; at Woolworth's request he incorporated numerous Gothic elements into the building.

❺ St Paul's Chapel St Paul's Chapel was completed in 1766 in a Georgian style, and George Washington worship-

CIVIC CENTER

Chambers St/
West Broadway

Cary Bldg.

Fire Department
Museum

J.K. Javits
Federal Bldg.

Irving Trust
Operation Center

Murray Bldg.

nan Sachs
quater
r constr.

New York
phone Bldg.

Chambers St/
Church St

New York City
Offices

Lafayette St.

Foley
Square

7 World
Trade Center

West Broadway

Greenwich St.

Park Pl.

Barclay St.

Church St.

Warren St.

Broadway

Chambers St.

Reade St.

Elk St.

Park St.

World Trade Center
(under constr.)

Federal Office
Bldg.

150 Broadway
Park Place

Murray St.

City Hall

Tweed
Courthouse

St. Andrew

World Trade Center Site
(Redevelopment in progress)
TC Memorial (under constr.)

St. Peter's

Woolworth
Building

City Hall

Park Row

Chambers St/
Center St

Park Row

Ground Zero

St. Paul's Chapel

CITY HALL PARK

Brooklyn Bridge/
City Hall

WTC

World Trade Center
PATH-Station

AT & T
Bldg.

Fulton St

Pace
University

Brooklyn
Bridge

Dey St.

Theater All.

Cortl. St.

Century
21

Western
Electric Bldg.

Nassau St.

Beekman
Hospital

Cortlandt St.

Fulton St/
Broadway

Fulton Street
Transit Center

Broadway-
Nassau/
Fulton St

Spruce St.

Beekman St.

Gold St.

Liberty
Bldg.

John St.

Ann St.

William St.

Nassau St.

Dutch St.

LIBERTY PLAZA
PARK

Maiden Ln.

St. John's
Methodist Church

Fulton St/
William St

Southbridge
Towers

American
ck Exchange

Trinity
Bldg.

Broadway

Liberty
St.

Liberty
Tower

Firefighter's
Museum

Trinity Church

Cedar St.

Federal
Reserve Bank

Gold St.

Pearl St.

Marine
Midland Bank

Chase Manhattan
Bank

Cliff St.

Fulton St.

Wall St/Broadway

Titanic
Memorial

Water St.

Canyon of Heroes

Federal Hall
Nat'l. Memorial

William St.

LOUISE
NEVELSON
PLAZA

Platt St.

Cannon's
Walk

Beekman St.

Broad St/Wall St

N. Y. Stock Exchange

Cedar St.

Maiden Ln.

SOUTH STREET
SEAPORT
(HISTORIC DIST.)

Shermerhorn Row

Fulton Market

U.S. Trust

Wall St/
William St

American International Bldg.

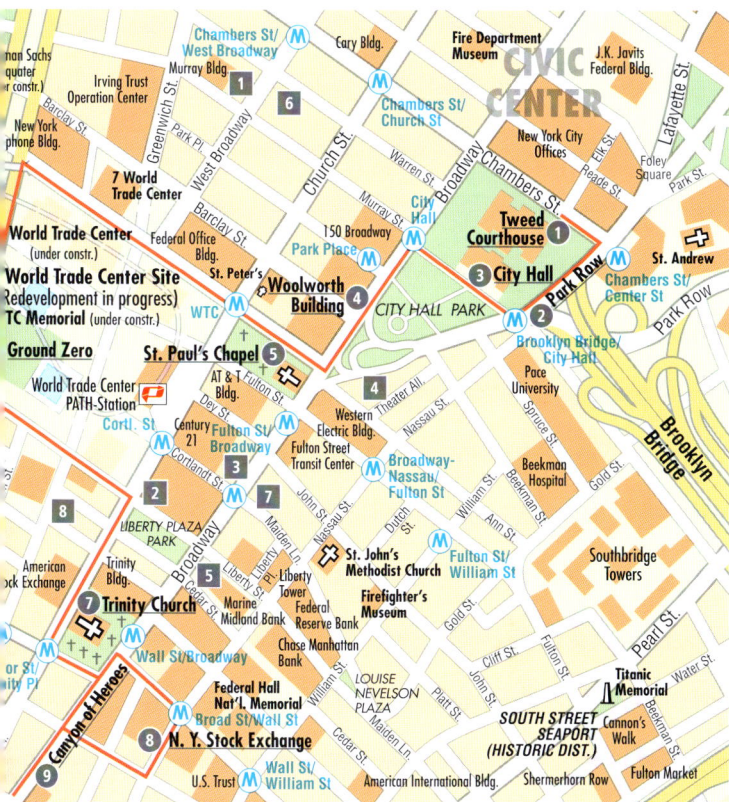

ped here after being sworn in as the first president. An oil painting of the U.S. coat of arms now hangs over the pew where he sat. An oak statue inside the church commemorates St Paul, the saint after whom the church is named.

⑥ Ground Zero In Church Street, on the exact spot where the famous Twin Towers of the World Trade Center rose into the sky before 11 September 2001, the day that changed the United States forever, is commemorated. The attack by

Islamist activists that transformed two scheduled planes into flying bombs, with all their passengers and crew, and wiped out so many lives, will never be forgotten. A "Wall of Heroes" commemorates the victims. In the plans for a new bulding

Babesta sells trendy clothes for cool kids.

the futurist design of the architect Daniel Libeskind was chosen. However, due to the financial crisis these plans were severely curtailed and are hardly recognizable from their original designs.

❼ Trinity Church The church was built of brown sandstone in the Gothic revival style in 1846. In the 19th century it was the tallest building in New York, although since then it has long been overshadowed by the skyscrapers in the Financial District. The bright stained-glass windows illuminate the high altar and the impressive bronze doors are decorated with Biblical scenes.

❽ New York Stock Exchange Founded in 1792 by several stockbrokers meeting under a plane tree on Wall Street to deal in state securities arising from the War of Independence, the NYSE is one of the most important stock exchanges in the world. Its current home, a building in the neo-classical style, was constructed in 1903. Chaos still seems to reign on its legendary trading floor of this political and economic power base beneath a vast skylight. The brass bells that signal the opening and closing of daily trading replaced the Chinese gong that was originally used.

❾ Canyon of Heroes The "Canyon of Heroes" is a stretch of Broadway in south Manhattan between Bowling Green and City Hall Park along which national heroes, such as astronauts and war veterans, are acclaimed with ticker-tape parades. The parades celebrating the end of World War II saw more than five thousand tons of paper rain down on the heads of the jubilant crowd.

SHOPPING

❶ Babesta Rock'n'roll parents (and their kids) are well looked-after at Jennifer Cattaui's store, which sells mini t-shirts with cool slogans or portraits of Mao and Kennedy. There are even CDs of rock songs re-recorded as lullabies. It's a trendy cornucopia and a great place to buy gifts to take home.
66 West Broadway (nahe Warren Street),
Tel 212-608-45 22,
www.babesta.com,
Mon–Fri 11.00–19.00,
Sat, Sun 1200–18.00.

❷ Brooks Brothers A respected source of classic gent's fashion wear for over a century. Even presidents have shopped here. The designer, Thom Brown, also caters for modern tastes with a slightly more forward-looking range.

Brooks Brothers is a destination store for men looking for formal business wear, as well as smart, but casual weekend wear.

1 Liberty Plaza,
Tel 212-267-24 00,
www.brooksbrothers.com,
Mon–Wed 8.00–19.00, Thurs
8.30–20.00, Fri 8.30–19.00, Sat
11.00–19.00, Sun 12.00–18.00.

3 Denim & Knits An insider tip for jeans' fans worldwide since 2007, stocking designer jeans and other denim products at giveaway prices.
2 Cortlandt Street (2nd floor),
Tel 212-571-26 00,
www.denimandknits.com,
Mon–Sat 10.00–20.00,
Sun 11.00–18.00.

4 J&R Music and Computer World A collection of stores with a wide selection of computers, cameras, stereos, and cell phones, but a word of caution for shoppers from abroad – North America runs on 120v current, so check the device you want will work at home before you buy it.
23 Park Row,
Tel 212-238-90 00,
www.jr.com,
Mon–Sat 9.00–19.30,
Sun 10.30–18.30.

EATING AND DRINKING

5 Alan's Falafel Alan's snack bar has long been an insider tip among the lunch crowd in New York's Financial District. His falafel (deep-fried chick-pea balls with herbs and spices) are a welcome alternative to hot dogs.
Cedar Street (Ecke Broadway), Tel 646-301-23 16,
Mon–Fri 7.00–16.00.

6 The Bigger Place Known as the "Little Place" before 9/11 and is now reborn under its new name. Tex-Mex food such as tacos and burritos, lovingly prepared. The signature dish here is blini (or Russian pancakes)
61 Warren Street
(at West Broadway),
Tel 212-528-31 75,
Mon–Fri 9.30–22.00,
Sat, Sun 9.00–16.00.

7 Mardigras Pizza The interior reminds you of carnival in New Orleans, and the spicy sauces and crayfish toppings on the pizzas remind you of Cajun cooking.
Maiden Lane (nahe Nassau Street), Tel 212-233-60 66,
Mon–Fri 10.30–21.00.

8 O'Hara's Restaurant Good-value Irish pub. The chicken fingers with honey mustard dip and the steak sandwiches are particularly tasty – as is the velvety Guinness on tap, of course.
120 Cedar Street,
Tel 212-267-3032,
Mon–Thurs 11.00–2.00,
Fri, Sat 11.00–4.00,
Sun 12.00–23.30.

With surface area of 101 x 53 m (331 x 174 ft) St Patrick´s Cathedral is one of the largest church buidings in the world.

SIGHTS

❶ Empire State Building The impressive Empire State Building, tapered toward the top, measures 381 m (1,250 ft) in height, or 449 m (1,473 ft) including the radio mast. For decades it was the tallest building in New York and it has always been (and still is) one of the most beautiful. The marble-clad shopping mall is bathed in art deco splendor just like the rest of the building, and the viewing platform guarantees astonishing views to visitors: a vast panorama unfolds in front of you, almost as if you were floating above Midtown. Building work began in 1930 and was completed in the record time of a little over a year, by a truly multicultural and hard-working group of construction workers, including Mohawk Native Americans known for their ability to work

in vertiginous heights. President Herbert Hoover opened the building on 1 May 1931. The skyscraper has featured in many films, including *King Kong* (1933), where King Kong famously hangs onto the outside of the building.

❷ New York Public Library A magnificent building, flanked by columns and housing some nine million books. In good weather, the entrance steps between the stone lions are popular with office folk as a place to take lunch.

❸ Grand Central Terminal The renovated in a Beaux Arts main station was opened in 1913 after several years of construction. The magnificent main hall is covered with an artificial sky depicting some 2,500 stars and the staircase borrowed style features from the one in the Paris Opera House.

❹ Times Square The legendary square is synonymous for many people with the pulsating life in New York. It is at the intersection of Broadway and Seventh Avenue between 42nd and 47th Streets. The area has been pedestrianized since 2009 and shopping is now as popular here as it always has been but more comfortable and less dangerous. There's the Virgin Megastore, aparently the largest record store in the world and themed restaurants such as the Official All Star Cafe of the U.S. sports elite. The dubious image and the seamy side have gone – to the regret of some fans who loved the New York of old.

❺ St Patrick's Cathedral Built in a neo-Gothic style between 1858 and 1879, the church is the seat of the Archbishop of New York and has shades of Cologne Cathedral,

N
0   200 m
0   600 feet

CENTRAL PARK

The Pond

Central Park South

THEATER DISTRICT

St. George

W. 56th St
W. 55th St
Eighth Ave

57th St
Arlen Bldg.

Carnegie Hall

Ed Sullivan

1700 Broadway Bldg.
Neil Simon
7th Ave. Bldg.

W. 58th St

City Center of Music and Dance

Burlington Bldg.

Broadway

Seventh Ave

7th Av

Winter Garden

50th St

49th St

J. C. Penny Bldg.

MGM Bldg.

ABC Bldg.

American Folk Art Mus.

American Mus. of Art & Design

Rockefeller Center

1 Rockefeller Plaza

47th-50th Sts
Rockefeller Center

Plaza Hotel

Pulitzer Fountain
Paris

W. 57th St

5th Ave. Church

Squibb Bldg.

MoMA Museum of Modern Art

Crown Bldg.

Austrian Cultural Forum

Zoo Wildlife Center
E. 64th St

Fifth Ave. Synagogue

E. 62nd St

E. 61st St

Madison Ave

Park Ave

E. 63rd St

Metropolitan Club

5th Av

E. 60th St

United Methodist

E. 59th St
Lexington Av

500 Park Tower

59th St

Trump Tower
Dahesh Museum

E. 58th St

E. 56th St

5th Av

Central Synagogue

E. 54th St

Lever House

E. 55th St

Top of the Rock
Rockefeller Plz.
NBC
Simon & Schuster Bldg.
British Empire Bldg.

Diamond Row

St. Patrick's Cathedral

Lexington Ave

Citigroup Center

ITT Bldg.
Colgate Palmolive Bldg.

Grolier Bldg.

MacMillan Bldg.

E. 53rd St

E. 52nd St

St. Bart's Church

Cort

Palace
St. Mary the Virgin
Fox Murdoch Bldg.
Stevens Tower

Duffy Square

Lyceum

Belasco

1166 Av. of the Americas

the Americas (6th Avenue)

Times Square

Times Sq
42nd St

Grace Bldg.

City University Graduate Sch.

W. 46th St

W. 45th St

W. 44th St

W. 41st St

42nd St

New York Public Library

American Standard Bldg.

W. 40th St

E. 41st St

Fifth Church

S & H Bldg.

W. 43rd St

Westvaco Bldg.

270 Park Ave

Chem. Bank Bldg.

American Brands Bldg.

Helmsley Bldg.

Life Met Bldg.

Grand Central Terminal

Whitney Mus. of American Art at Altria
42nd St
Grand Central

MIDTOWN

Park Ave

800 3rd Ave. Bldg.

E. 51st St

E. 50th St

E. 49th St

E. 48th St

E. 47th St

E. 46th St

E. 45th St

Church of the Holy Family

Second Ave

Third Ave

GARMENT DISTRICT

E. 39th St

E. 38th St

E. 37th St

Lord & Taylor

Mid-Manhattan Library

Madison Ave

E. 40th St

Chrysler Bldg.

Charin Bldg.

E. 44th St

E. 43rd St

E. 42nd St

Mobil Bldg.

2 UN Plaza

1 UN Plaza

United Nations Headquarters

United Nations Plz.

E. 35th St
E. 34th St

Fifth Ave

Empire State Building

Morgan Library & Museum

Scandinavia House

Park Ave

MURRAY HILL

Our Saviour

101 Park Ave

Continental Group Bldg.

Daily News

Ford Foundation Bldg.

Tudor City

Burroughs Bldg.

TUDOR

Tudor City Pl.

With a starry clientele, the Plaza Hotel is still one of the most luxurious hotels in the world.

although it is of course medieval only in its look. Nevertheless the church features an almost grotesque contrast between the Gothic and modernity, making it rather special. Standing in amongst the magnificent skyscrapers of Fifth Avenue the cathedral seems almost forlorn – yet nevertheless an important landmark of New York.

6 **Rockefeller Center** Originally built between 1930 and 1940 at the behest of the oil magnate John D. Rockefeller Jr, the complex is now composed of 21 interlinked skyscrapers housing many offices, television studios, restaurants, stores, and an ice rink. A highlight is the Radio City Music Hall, once a cinema, in which concerts and other events are now held.

7 **Lever House** Designed by the architect Gordon Bunshaft,

this office block on Park Avenue is a perfect example of 1950s International Style architecture and has been listed as a national monument since October 1983. Its name is a legacy from the British pharmaceutical manufacturer Lever Brothers, who once had their headquarters here.

8 **Trump Tower** This exclusive apartment block has a spectacular atrium and a mall two floors high with many boutiques. There is a waterfall that flows down seven floors and the façade of this impressive building is clad in bronze glass sheets.

9 **Plaza Hotel** The legendary New Yorker luxury hotel on Central Park was built in the early years of the 20th century. The complex was built to the designs of Henry J. Hardenbergh in the French Renais-

sance style and opened in 1907. Right from the start it was regarded as one of the best hotels in the world. A famous regular was the great writer and Nobel Prize winner Ernest Hemingway.

SHOPPING

1 **Tiffany & Co.** This upscale shop will always be linked with the film *Breakfast at Tiffany's*, in which Audrey Hepburn admired the company's fine jewels, and many visitors do the same today. Less costly souvenirs in Tiffany gift bags are also available.
727 Fifth Ave (near 57th Street), Tel 212-755-80 00, www.tiffany.com, Mon–Sat 10.00–19.00, Sun 12.00–18.00.

2 **FAO Schwarz** A children's paradise of a toy shop with a huge stock of mass-produced

Tiffany & Co. in Fifth Avenue is a definite must-see on every shopping trip to New York.

toys and hand-made collector's pieces. The Christmas window displays are worth seeing.
767 Fifth Ave (near 58th Street), Tel 212-644-94 00, www.fao.com, Mon–Thurs 10.00–19.00, Fri, Sat 10.00–20.00, Sun 11.00–18.00.

3 Niketown Five floors of trendy Nike products. Sportswear from tracksuits to sweatbands and trainers with built-in iPods await your visit.
6 E 57th Street (near Fifth Ave), Tel 212-891-64 53, www.nike.com, Mon–Sat 10.00–20.00, Sun 11.00– 19.00.

4 Saks Fifth Avenue One of Manhattan's best-known department stores since 1924. For many well-off New Yorkers, this iconic temple to consumerism is still the place to shop.
611 Fifth Ave (near 50th St),

Tel 212-753-40 00, www.saksfifthavenue.com, Mon–Fri 10.00–20.00, Sat 10.00– 19.00, Sun 12.00–19.00.

EATING AND DRINKING

5 Daniel An excellent restaurant, which mixes home cooking with gourmet fare and is famed for its innovative "French country cuisine". The opulent décor may take a bit of getting used to.
60 E 65th Street (near Fifth Avenue), Tel 288-00 33, www.danielnyc.com, Mon–Thurs 17.45–23.00, Fri, Sat 17.30–23.00.

6 Hatsuhana The delicate raw fish, served on Hawaiian leaves, really melts in the mouth. It's best to try the sushi chef's recommendations.
237 Park Ave (near 46th Street), Tel 212-661-34 00,

www.hatsuhana.com, Mon–Fri 11.45–14.45, 17.30–22.00.

7 Grand Central Oyster Bar The oyster bar located in the basement of Grand Central Terminal has long been a New York fixture. The oysters, the clam chowder, and the other fish dishes are delicious.
Grand Central Station, 89 E 42nd Street, Tel 212-490-66 50, www.oysterbarny.com, Mon–Fri 11.30–21.30, Sat 12.00–21.30.

8 Brasserie An American ambience with large video screens and the finest French bistro cuisine. The onion soup is authentic and the delicious chocolate beignets delicious.
100 E 53rd Street (near Park Ave), Tel 212-751-48 40, Sun–Thurs 11.00–24.00, Fri, Sat 11.00–1.00.

With its neo-classical columns the Vanderbilt House resembles a country manor.

SIGHTS

❶ Vanderbilt House A gigantic brick and limestone townhouse with red tiles located on the south-east corner of Fifth Avenue and 86th Street, built in 1914 and bought in 1944 for the wife of millionaire Cornelius Vanderbilt IV. Generations of Vanderbilts lived off the enormous fortune amassed, not always entirely legally, by Cornelius, the "railroad king", in the 19th century.

❷ Jackie Onassis's Home Jacqueline "Jackie" Bouvier Kennedy Onassis lived on the 15th floor of the building at 1040 Fifth Avenue on the Upper East Side. The glamorous lady bought the penthouse soon after the assassination of her husband, President John F. Kennedy, and she lived there until her own death in 1994. Jackie loved New York and en-

joyed jogging unrecognized in the area of Central Park close to her home, especially around the reservoir that now bears her name.

❸ Benjamin Duke's Home The former residence, built in 1901, of Benjamin Duke is located on the corner of Fifth Avenue and 82nd Street. Duke and his younger brother James originally came from North Carolina and founded the American Tobacco Company. They endowed a small college, which was later to be expanded into Duke University.

❹ NYU Graduate School of Art History A magnificent building located on the corner of Fifth Avenue and 78th Street, based in style on a typical chateau in the Bordeaux area in France, and praised by several critics as "one of the most beautiful mansions in

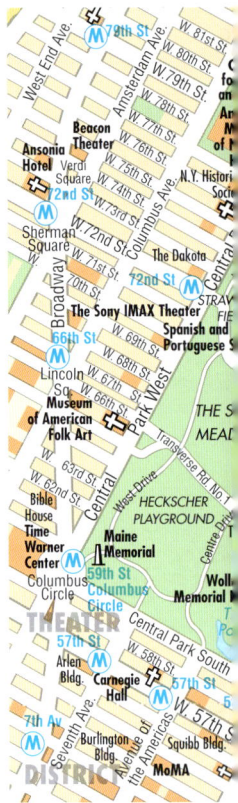

New York". Benjamin Duke's widow and his daughter (see 3 above) lived at this grand building up until the late 1950s, leaving the estate to New York University; it now houses the NYU Graduate School of Art History.

Congregation
Rodeph Sholom

Jacqueline
Kennedy
Onassis
Reservoir

THE GREAT
st St | useum of Natural History
LAWN

Guggenheim
Museum

Neue
Galerie

1 Vanderbilt House

Jackie Onassis's Home

Turtle Pond

Metropolitan
Museum of Art

Park Ave
Synagogue

Goethe
Institute

86th St

3 Benjamin Duke's Home

THE RAMBLE

YORKVILLE

Transverse Rd. N.

Statue of Alice
in Wonderland

Statue of
Ch. Andersen

4 NYU Graduate School of Art History

77th St

5 Pulitzer House

Whitney Museum
of American Art

Temple
Shaaray Tefila

6 Frick Collection

Asia Society

Hellenic
Cathedral

Gracie Square
Hospital

Temple
Emanu-El

Light Opera
of Manhattan

8 Home of Ulysses S. Grant

UPPER
EAST SIDE

7 Roosevelt Twin Town House

Sotheby's

Park East
Synagogue

N.Y. Hospital
Cornell Medical
Center

Memorial
Sloan Kettering
Cancer Center

Rockefeller
University

**8 Lexington
Av.**

Manhattan Ear
& Throat Hosp.

University
Hospital

J.H.Holmers
Towers

Doctor's
(Beth Israel)
Hospital

Gracie mansion
(Mayor's House)

CARL
SCHURZ
PARK

Bird S. Coler
Memorial Hospital

Octagon
Tower

OCTAGON
PARK

ROOSEVELT

Roosevelt Island
Public School

Roosevelt Island
Bridge

ISLAND

West Channel

East Channel

Franklin D. Roosevelt Drive

JOHN JAY
PARK

N
200 m
600 feet

5 Pulitzer House A magnificent building on East 73rd Street between Fifth and Madison Avenue, and once the home of Joseph Pulitzer (1847–1911). A Hungarian who emmigrated to the United States in his youth, he joined the Unionist army and fought in the Civil War. After the war he became one of the most successful publishers in the United States and the Pulitzer Prize is named after him. Nowadays 13 residents live behind the decorative columns. Pulitzer, who was extremely sensitive to noise, actually spent very little time there, despite having a soundproof room built.

6 Frick Collection Henry Clay Frick's mansion takes up a whole block between 70th and

Frick Collection: if you only have time to visit one gallery, this has some of the finest paintings in the art world.

71st Streets. A millionaire several times over who had made his fortune in steel, his art collection concentrated on Italian Renaissance painting. Thomas Hastings, his architect, who had also designed the New York Public Library, was charged from the outset to design the house as a museum and gallery that would be opened to the public. Frick bequeathed his art treasures to a trust, which converted the private apartments into a museum after his death and that of his wife, opening them to the general public in 1935. The Frick Collection holds works of art dating from the 12th to the late 19th century, including canvases from the Italian Renaissance period, France, 18th-century England, and 17th-century Holland. The Frick Collection is one of the most important art collections in New York.

❼ Roosevelt Twin Town House The two houses at 47–49 East 65th Street had only one door to the street and belonged to Franklin D. Roosevelt, who was first elected American president in 1932 and then went on to become the only president to be re-elected three times. The house was lived in by the president and his mother, and now belongs to Hunter College.

❽ Home of Ulysses S. Grant Ulysses S. Grant lived in this building at 3 East 66th Street opposite Central Park between 1881 and 1885. The legendary Civil War general held office as president of the United States between 1869 and 1877, but was rather less successful as a politician, his period of office being overshadowed by several corruption scandals. Suffering from terminal cancer, the ex-president wrote his memoirs, which were to enjoy great success, in his house at Central Park.

SHOPPING

❶ Barneys New York You see it one day on a film star – and the next it's avalable at Barneys New York: this temple to designer fashion is located in one of the most expensive areas of the East Side and stints neither on its exclusive offers nor its prices. Exceptional cosmetics department.
660 Madison Ave,
Tel 212-826-89 00,
www.barneys.com,
Mon–Fri 10.00–20.00,
Sat 10.00–19.00,
Sun 11.00– 18.00.

❷ La Maison du Chocolat Who says there's no good chocolate in America? This is first-class quality from Paris, served in a branch of the

Best Cellars: quality wines at a reasonable price, for every taste bud and every wallet.

famous French chocolatier. Excellent homemade pralines, imaginative flavorings, and delightful gift ideas.
1018 Madison Ave,
Tel 212-744-71 17,
www.lamaisonduchocolat.com,
Mon–Sat 10.00–19.00, Sun
12.00–18.00.

3 **Artbag** Wide selection of beautiful designer purses, handbags, and other leather goods has been serving New Yorkers for more than 60 years. Everything from a coin purse to a sturdy rucksack.
130 Madison Ave,
Tel 212-744-27 20,
www.artbag.com,
Mon–Fri 9.30–17.00, Sat
10.00–16.00.

4 **Best Cellars** This cellar is well named – the wines on its wooden shelves are first-class and good value into the bargain, with no bottle costing

more than $15. The bottles are divided into such categories as "soft" and "juicy".
1291 Lexington Ave
(nahe 86th Street),
Tel 212-426-42 00,
www.bestcellars.com,
Mon–Thurs 9.30–21.00,
Fri, Sat 9.30–22.00,
Sun 12.00– 20.00.

EATING AND DRINKING

5 **Cafe Boulud** Pepped-up homemade food at affordable prices. French country cuisine, vegetarian food, and seasonal dishes. The fish dishes are good.
20 E 76th Street,
Tel 212-772-26 00,
www.danielnyc.com,
17.45–23.00, daily,
Tues–Sat 12.00–14.30.

6 **Nick's Family-Style Restaurant and Pizzeria** Since 2003, Nick Angelis has been serving up his popular dishes

on the Upper East Side. Fresh tomato sauce, homemade mozzarella, and fine vegetables make for pleasant dining.
1814 Second Ave,
Tel 212-987-57 00,
11.30–22.00, daily.

7 **Paola's** Paola has been a reassuring presence here for 12 years, serving classic Italian dishes and first-class wines.
245 E 84th Street,
Tel 212-794-18 90,
www.paolasrestaurant.com,
Sun–Wed 17.00–22.00,
Thurs–Sat 17.00–23.00.

8 **Park Avenue Summer** This consistently good restaurant reinvents itself every year.
100 E 63rd Street (corner
Park Ave), Tel 212-644-19 00,
www.parkavenyc.com,
Mon–Fri 11.30–15.00, Sat, Sun
from 11.00, Mon–Thurs 17.30–
23.00, Fri, Sat to 23.30,
Sun to 22.00.

The American Museum of Natural History welcomes three million visitors each year.

SIGHTS

❶ Children's Museum of Manhattan An exemplary "hands-on" museum where children can learn the secrets of the earth and everyday life through interactive exhibits and play. Changing displays show how amusement park rollercoasters and roundabouts work, and smaller visitors can play at being police officers and firefighters in toy towns. Birthday parties can also be booked here. If you are visiting New York en famille, spend some time here. The kids will have a great time.

❷ Ansonia Hotel Financed by William Earle Dodge Stokes, a rich mine owner, the Ansonia Hotel, located at the intersection of Broadway and Amsterdam Avenue, was built between 1899 and 1904 as one of the Upper West Side's first luxury hotels. It was also one of the first to benefit from the luxury of air-conditioning. The singer Enrico Caruso and the baseball star Babe Ruth both spent long periods staying at the hotel.

❸ Beresford Building This monumental palazzo is one of Manhattan's most elegant addresses. Designed by the master architect Emery Roth, the three towers on the roof have become the building's trademark. Various façades and decorations help to mask the building's rather solid appearance. The Beresford replaced the six-floor Hotel Beresford, which was built in 1889 by Alva Walker. Several billionaires now live in the luxurious apartments.

❹ Rose Center for Earth and Space The American Museum of Natural History houses a four-floor planetarium. Narrated by the Hollywood star Harrison Ford, the space show *Are We Alone?* uses sensational special effects in an unusual way to demonstrate the view that we cannot be the only living beings in the

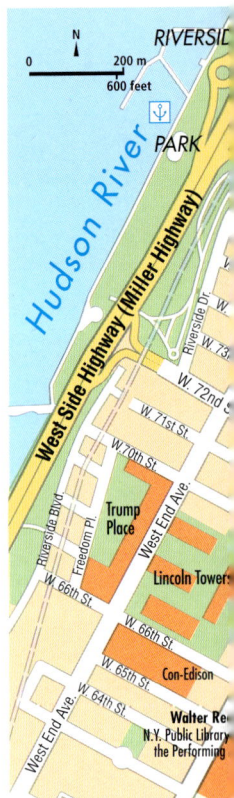

Map labels:

W. 87th St.
W. 86th St.
W. 86th St.
86th St Ⓜ
Jaqueline Kennedy Onassis Reservoir
West End Ave.
West Drive
Edgar Allan Poe St. (W. 84th St.)
W. 85th St.
W. 86th Transverse Rd.

① Children's Museum of Manhattan

⑤
⑦
②
W. 83rd St.
W. 82nd St.
Amsterdam Ave.
Columbus Ave.
Congregation Rodeph Sholom
Central Park West

9th St.
Ⓜ 79th St.
W. 79th St.
W. 81st St.
W. 80th St.
④

③ Beresford Building
Ⓜ 81st St–Museum of Natural History
THE GREAT LAWN

W. 78th St.
St
W. 77th St.
④ Rose Center for Earth and Space

⑤ American Museum of Natural History
Delacorte Theater
Cleopatra's Needle
Belvedere Castle
Turtle Pond
East Drive

⑥
Ansonia Hotel
Verdi Square
W. 76th St.
W. 77th St.

② 72nd St
⑥ New York Historical Society
W. 75th St.
W. 79th Transverse Rd.
Metropolitan Museum of Art

③
W. 74th St.
W. 73rd St.
THE RAMBLE
CENTRAL PARK
The Lake

⑦ Dakota Building
W. 71st St.
West Drive
Bow Bridge
Boathouse Restaurant

Ⓜ 72nd St
SONY IMAX
W. 70th St.
Spanish and Portuguese Synagogue
Central Park West
Columbus Ave.
W. 69th St.
⑧ Strawberry Fields
Statue of Alice in Wonderland
Fifth Ave.
Harkness House

W. 68th St.
Cherry Hill Fountain
Statue of H. Ch. Andersen
E. 74st St.

①
W. 67th St.
In Museum of American Folk Art
Bethesda Fountain
Pavilion
Conservatory Pond

---

universe. The *Cosmic Pathway* illustrates some 15 billion years of space history.

⑤ American Museum of Natural History Covering four city blocks, the largest natural history museum in the world is located on the corner of Central Park and 79th Street; its 46 exhibition halls house more than 35 million exhibits. The building was constructed between 1874 and 1899 to a design by Calvert Vaux and Jacob Wrey Mould and is reminiscent of ancient Roman triumphal buildings. The collection of dinosaur skeletons is one of the main attractions for young and old alike and includes Barosaurus lentus, one of the world's largest dinosaurs. The Hall of Ocean Life has an

The Beatles' song *Strawberry Fields* penned by John Lennon refers to an orphanage with this name in Liverpool.

impressive 30-m (100-ft) long skeleton of a blue whale and the Hall of Minerals and Gems boasts the Star of India, the world's largest sapphire.

6 New York Historical Society The society was founded in 1804 and has set itself the task of conserving the history of the city by placing it in context to the present. There is a library and an archive with newspapers, manuscripts, and other documents available for research purposes, and the history of New York comes to life in the museum next door.

7 Dakota Building The Dakota is one of the finest apartment buildings in New York. It was built in a German Renaissance style between 1880 and 1884 by Henry J. Hardenbergh, and has often been compared to a Hanseatic town hall. One legend has it that

Edward Clark, the boss of the Singer Sewing Machine Company who commissioned the building, named it after the American states North and South Dakota, as the Upper West Side was still outside the city at the time and almost as far away from Manhattan as the Dakotas. The suites have been home to such celebrities as Judy Garland, Leonard Bernstein, and John Lennon, who was shot dead by a crazed fan outside the Dakota Building on 8 December 1980.

8 Strawberry Fields Strawberry Fields in Central Park is a memorial to John Lennon and his song of that name. The area was officially listed as "Strawberry Fields" on 26 March 1981 and Lennon's widow, Yoko Ono, donated $1 million to the Central Park Conservancy for the creation and upkeep of the site. The focus of the

memorial site is a mosaic, made by Italian craftsmen from Naples – in the center is the word *Imagine* from one of Lennon's most famous songs.

SHOPPING

1 Barnes & Noble Superstore The biggest chain of bookstores in the United States, a "book supermarket" that offers more than just the titles in the bestseller list. There are attractive price reductions on older books, often soon after publication. *1972 Broadway, Tel 212-595-68 59, www.barnesandnoble.com, 9.00–24.00, daily.*

2 Westsider Rare & Used Books This shop is famed for its wide range of second-hand books, current novels, and reference works, often at half price. The valuable and expensive

Barnes & Noble is a paradise for bookworms, offering plenty of books to get their teeth into.

first editions are to be found on the upper floor.
2246 Broadway,
Tel 212-362-07 06,
www.westsiderbooks.com,
10.00–24.00, daily.

3 Crocs A shop devoted to Crocs? Only in the Big Apple. But once you've entered the shop and seen the almost inexhaustible range and variety of these plastic clogs you'll realize just how much is included under the name Crocs. Okay – they've got flip-flops as well.
270 Columbus Ave,
Tel 212-362-16 55.

4 Maxilla & Mandible This natural history knick-knack shop has unusual stones and shells from all over the world, illuminated butterflies in little wooden boxes, fossils, and toys for the little ones.
451 Columbus Ave,
Tel 212-724-61 73,
www.maxillaand mandible.com,
Mon–Sat 11.00–19.00,
Sun 11.00–17.00.

EATING AND DRINKING

5 Zabar's The enormous selection of delicatessen and generously filled sandwiches will satisfy even the most demanding palate. This gourmet paradise has – quite rightly – been voted the best deli in the city on several occasions.
2245 Broadway (Ecke 80th Street), Tel 212-787-20 00,
www.zabars.com,
Mon–Fri 8.00–19.30, Sat 8.00–20.00, Sun 19.00–18.00.

6 Josie's West Healthy food doesn't have to be boring, as Louis Lanza, the head chef of this first-class health food restaurant has proven.
300 Amsterdam Ave,
Tel 212-769-12 12,
www.josiesnyc.com,
Mon–Thurs 12.00–23.00, Fri 12.00–24.00, Sat 11.00–24.00, Sun 10.30–22.30.

7 H & H This bagel bakery is a New York institution. The bagels, which are traditionally especially good with cream cheese and smoked salmon, arrive fresh and warm from the oven every few minutes.
2239 Broadway,
Tel 212-595-80 03,
www.hhbagels.net

8 Fairway Market Fresh meat, seafood, delicious appetizers, sandwiches, and other tempting pastry bites are just some of the highlights at this gourmet market. The café and steakhouse are also worth visiting – an insider tip.
2127 Broadway (corner 74th Street), Tel 212-595-18 88,
www.fairwaymarket.com,
6.00–1.00, daily.

The NYC Transit Museum displays model trains as well as real carriages.

SIGHTS

❶ Prospect Park This park in the heart of Brooklyn was designed by Frederick Law Olmsted and Calvert Vaux, who were also responsible for Central Park, and it has been a popular destination for excursions since 1866. There are extensive meadows and paths through this green oasis; you can go skating at the Kate Wollman Rink, and Grand Army Plaza has the Soldiers' and Sailors' Monument for the fallen of the Civil War.

❷ Flatbush Avenue Brooklyn's main artery runs between Manhattan Bridge and Jamaica Bay, following an old Native North American path. Long Island University, Fulton Mall, the Brooklyn Academy of Music, the Brooklyn Public Library, Brooklyn Botanic Garden, and Prospect Park are all to be found along this road, which has four lanes for much of its length. Immortalized in many songs, Flatbush Avenue is also one of New York's busiest roads.

❸ New York City Transit Museum This little museum, located in an old subway station, has historic trains that would have rattled through New York at the turn of the 20th century, as well as photos, tickets, old subway maps, and other exhibits illustrating the history of the world's largest underground network.

❹ Brooklyn Historical Society The Museum of the Brooklyn Historical Society is an informative recapitulation of the history of Brooklyn, bringing the narrative of this area to life with historic films, photos, and other documents; changing special exhibitions concentrate on various topics. The four-floor building was designed by the architect George B. Post and built in Queen Anne style in 1881; the façade has impressively ornate terracotta reliefs. It was listed in 1991.

❺ Willow Street The three brownstone houses at Nos. 155 to 157 Willow Street are among the most beautiful and interesting buildings from the so-called Federal period, which lasted from the War of Independence to the 1830s. During this time architects tended to restrict themselves to simple façades showing little if any decoration. Since the course of Willow Street has been altered, the houses on it now no longer run parallel to the street. A tunnel runs from the cellar of one of the houses to what used to be a stable but is now a residential house. The

Brooklyn Bridge

Fulton
Ferry
Landing

**Brooklyn
Heights
Promenade**

BROOKLYN
HEIGHTS
HISTORIC
DISTRICT

**Brooklyn Historical
Society**

**New York City
Transit Museum**

Brooklyn Navy Yard

Navy
Yard
Basin

N

0   200 m
600 feet

COMMODORE
BARRY
PARK

Cumberland
Hospital

FORT
GREENE
PARK

Long Island
Univ.

Brooklyn
Hospital

Brooklyn
Academy
of Music

Flatbush Ave.
Station

SOUTH
BROOKLYN

WYCKOFF
GARDENS

Holy Family
Hospital

CARROLL
PARK

GOWANUS

JAMES J. BYRNE
MEMORIAL
PARK & PLGD.

Gowanus
House

Grand Army
Plaza

Grand Army
Plaza

Prospect Park

The Fulton Ferry Landing, in the shadow of the Brooklyn Bridge.

famous writer Truman Capote once lived in the 11-bedroom mansion at 70 Willow Street.

❻ Fulton Ferry Landing Before the construction of the Brooklyn Bridge in 1883 and the Manhattan Bridge in 1909, ferries used to travel between the independent City of Brooklyn and Manhattan, known then as the City of New York. Fulton Ferry, the ferry stop on the Brooklyn side, was named after Robert Fulton, who built the first steamship and ran the ferry service; the last ferry ran in 1924 and now only water taxis stop here. The streets on both sides of East River leading to the ferry stops are called Fulton Street.

❼ Brooklyn Heights Promenade This romantic district with lots of historic brownstones and townhouses lies at the mouth of the East River

and was a stopping point for the ferry to Manhattan in the 19th century. Sunset over New York is at its most beautiful seen from Fulton Landing. Truman Capote and Arthur Miller both lived on Willow Street and bustling Atlantic Avenue, known as "Little Arabia", is famous for its spice stores. The views of the Manhattan skyline from Brooklyn Promenade on the shores of the East River are considered the very best.

❽ Brooklyn Bridge One of the landmarks of the city, the venerable structure fits harmoniously into the cityscape despite its neo-Gothic shapes. The initial designs for the bridge were undertaken by the German architect John August Roebling and was the first suspension bridge in the world to use steel cable stays. Shortly after its inauguration in 1883, the structure connecting Man-

hattan and Brooklyn experienced a mass panic because of an unfortunate accident and 35 people died. Luckily no similar accident ever occurred. It celebrated its 125th anniversary in 2008, and today the popular bridge still serves its original purpose as a traffic route, and continues to be a major New York City icon.

SHOPPING

▌ Heights Books An antiquarian bookstore with an exquisite stock of science books and reference works, and especially popular with academics. Thi is also a favourite shop for specialist book enthusiasts. Art lovers will also find a good selection of art books.
109 Montague Street,
Tel 718-624-48 76,
http://heightsbooks.com,
Sun–Thurs 11.00–23.00,
Fri, Sat 11.00–24.00.

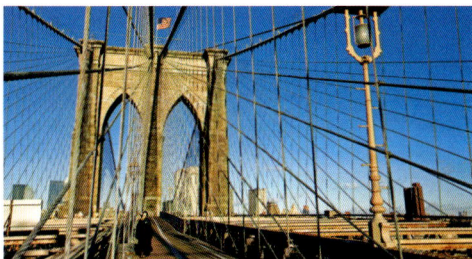

A walk across the Brooklyn Bridge provides you with great views of the port and toward the other bridges in the north.

2 Tango One of the few boutiques still in family ownership. Businesswomen buy designer suits, dresses, and fine quality leisurewear here. This is the place if you are looking for a suit tio wear t an important job interview.
145 Montague Street,
Tel 718-625-7518,
Mon–Fri 10.30– 19.30, Sat 10.30–18.30, Sun 12.30–18.00.

3 Overtures The store is best known for its excellent paper; there is writing paper of every quality and shade here, and you can have it headed, of course. Lovers of stationery will be in heaven.
216 Hicks Street,
Tel 718-643-93 45,
Mon–Fri 10.30–19.00,
Sat, Sun 11.00–18.30.

4 St Mark's Comics Comic collectors from all over the world come here to shop.

An almost inexhaustible selection of comics to suit every comic fan.
148 Montague Street,
Tel 718-935-09 11,
www.stmarkscomics.com,
Mon, Tues 10.00– 23.00,
Wed–Sat 10.00–21.00,
Sun 11.00–19.00.

EATING AND DRINKING

5 Brooklyn Ice Cream Factory Mark Thompson's ice cream, available in eight classic flavors, is famed for its pure taste and creamy consistency.
The Corner of Old Fulton/Water Street, Tel 718-246-39 63, Thurs–Sun 12.00–22.00.

6 Grimaldi's Pizzeria Loud and very hectic, but the pizzas from the wood oven taste so good the noise won't put you off. It has become something of an New York institution in the pizza world.

19 Old Fulton Street,
Tel 718-858-43 00,
www.grimaldis.com,
Mon–Thurs 11.30–22.45, Fri 11.30–22.45, Sat 12.00–23.45, Sun 12.00–22.45.

7 Jacques Torres Chocolate This little chocolatier is a paradise for every chocolate fan. Torres' amazing creations lay to rest the tale that there is no decent chocolate in America.
66 Water Street,
Tel 718-875-97 72,
www.mrchocolate.com,
Mon–Sat 9.00–19.00,
Sun 10.00–18.00.

8 Superfine Restaurant Laura Taylor, the chef, serves up Mediterranean cuisine, especially excellent fish.
126 Front Street,
Tel 718-243-90 05,
Tues–Fri 11.30–15.00, 18.00– 23.00, Sat 15.00– 23.00, Sun 11.00–15.00, 18.00–22.00.

INDEX

PICTURE CREDITS/IMPRINT

MONACO BOOKS is an imprint of Verlag Wolfgang Kunth
© Verlag Wolfgang Kunth GmbH & Co.KG, Munich, 2011
Concept: Wolfgang Kunth
Editing and design: Verlag Wolfgang Kunth GmbH&Co.KG
English translation/editing: Silva Editions Ltd.; JMS Books LLP

For distribution please contact:
Monaco Books
c/o Verlag Wolfgang Kunth, Königinstr.11
80539 München, Germany
Tel: +49 / 89/45 80 20 23
Fax: +49 / 89/ 45 80 20 21
info@kunth-verlag.de
www.monacobooks.com
www.kunth-verlag.de

NOTES

NOTES

NOTES

NOTES

NOTES

NOTES

NOTES